GOVERNMENT
AND THE
GOVERNED

DOUGLAS WASS

GOVERNMENT AND THE GOVERNED

BBC REITH LECTURES 1983

Routledge & Kegan Paul
London, Boston, Melbourne and Henley

First published in book form in 1984
by Routledge & Kegan Paul plc

39 Store Street, London WC1E 7DD, England

9 Park Street, Boston, Mass. 02108, USA

464 St Kilda Road, Melbourne,
Victoria 3004, Australia and

Broadway House, Newtown Road,
Henley-on-Thames, Oxon RG9 1EN, England

Set in Sabon 11/13pt
by Columns, Reading
and printed in Great Britain
by Billing & Sons Ltd, Worcester

Library of Congress Cataloging in Publication Data

Wass, Douglas, Sir, 1923-

Government and the governed.
(BBC Reith lectures; 1983)
1. Great Britain—Politics and government—1979- —
Addresses, essays, lectures. 2. Political participation—
Great Britain—Addresses, essays, lectures. I. Title.
II. Series: B.B.C. Reith lectures; 1983.
JN231.W34   1984   354.41   83-26877

British Library CIP data available

ISBN 0-7102-0312-8
ISBN 0-7102-0316-0 (pbk.)

Contents

Preface

This book consists of the texts I used in delivering the Reith Lectures which were transmitted by the BBC in the United Kingdom and abroad in the winter of 1983-4. The language used and the style assumed were what I judged the medium of radio to require from someone seeking to engage the interest of a wide audience in a serious subject of public concern. Neither the language nor the style would have been the same had I been composing my thoughts for the written, not the spoken word. Nor would the length of the texts have been identical. I was constrained to thirty minutes of speech for each of the six lectures.

Other authors of the Reith Lectures have judged that the differences between the medium of speech and that of writing, and the time constraints of radio demanded that they rewrite the lectures for book publication. I was myself initially tempted to do this. But I decided that, having cast my lectures very deliberately in a form for radio transmission, it was worth preserving them in precisely that form.

I received much helpful advice and criticism from half a dozen or so people who saw the lectures in draft at one stage or another. I will not embarrass them by naming them; but they will recognise in these few words my sense of obligation to them for the trouble they took to help me.

One person who helped me cannot, however, remain anonymous. This is the producer of the lectures, Mr David Morton of the BBC. His assistance to me in turning a raw and barely serviceable script into something that could actually be disseminated to a mass audience was beyond price; and his patience and perseverance in educating me in the use of the microphone seem in retrospect to have had no limits. If the lectures have had any wide appeal, much of the credit must go to him. Their imperfections however are uniquely my own.

Douglas Wass
December 1983

LECTURE I

United Thoughts
and Counsels

Ten days after I accepted the invitation of the Governors of the BBC to give this year's Reith Lectures, I found myself almost by chance in the Palazzo Pubblico in Siena, admiring two well-preserved frescoes painted by Ambrogio Lorenzetti. In one, the very depiction of misery and punitive chastisement, the people who inhabit the painting cringe in fear, bedraggled and impoverished. The title 'Bad Government'. In the other, entitled 'Good Government', we see prosperity, blue skies, fields rich with crops, the citizens going about their business in the epitome of Arcadian contentment. Why, I asked myself, did Lorenzetti entitle these murals as he did, and not, for instance, 'Poverty' and 'Prosperity'? What is it about good government that he equated with well-being? It may seem strange that the permanent secretary to the Treasury, as I then was, should be putting this question to himself, for the identity of good government and prosperity has been taken for granted for a long time. Herodotus tells us how Lycurgus, following an inspired visit to the Oracle at Delphi, in the seventh or eighth century BC, brought good government to Sparta, reorganised the army, and introduced the new civil

3

offices of Ephor and Elder. Thereafter the Laced-aemonians, as he put it, 'soon shot up and flourished like a sturdy tree'.

In our own times, too, many of us have come to link the government with our material prosperity. General elections are fought on what is described as the government's economic performance. And our disappointing post-war achievements compared with some of our neighbours are laid by some people at the very door of government.

Are we right, I wonder, and is history right to equate good government with prosperity and bad government with poverty? And when we talk about government what do we mean? Are we referring to the system, to the component parts of the political and administrative machinery? Or do we mean the policies which governments try to follow? Many of the attributes of a good system of government have been recognised for centuries. The provision of a clear legal code with an accessible judicial system; an executive free from corruption backed up by an efficient civil and military service; perhaps a consultative or legislative assembly.

You will notice that good government, so construed, does not necessarily involve popular participation. There is nothing in Lorenzetti's paintings to suggest that the ordinary citizens in fourteenth-century Italy had any voice in the making of the laws or in the design of the foreign policy of the prince who ruled over them. Perhaps the thought never occurred to them that good government had anything to do with democracy. The Athenians however would not have accepted this disjunction. And nor will we. For us, as for them, the essence of good government is that it should be democratic. *Vox populi, vox dei.*

As I pondered over the essential requirements of a good system of government I found I could narrow them down to two ideas: efficiency and responsiveness. It may seem odd to elevate efficiency to such a level of importance in considering anything so fundamental to the human condition as government, but I am using the term in a very broad sense. For me efficiency means that actions and decisions are taken in a rational and systematic way; that internal conflicts and inconsistencies are brought to the surface and resolved; and that objectives are defined and optimal means employed to secure them.

The wish that government should be both efficient and responsive can also be seen to be a corollary of the thinking of the political philosophers who have shaped and moulded our society since the seventeenth century. The rise of liberalism as a political creed in this country stemmed essentially from the writing of John Locke, who argued, even before Adam Smith, that commerce and the free competitive market provided the citizen with the greatest opportunity to promote his own and society's welfare. The market was identified as an efficient mechanism for providing goods and services, and a mechanism too which responded to consumer preferences. Producers who were inefficient were displaced by those who were not. Those who failed to meet the consumer's wishes were likewise displaced by those who gave them satisfaction.

But there is a wide area of our society and economy where market forces do not, indeed cannot, operate. This is the area of government itself. For good or ill modern government is big – not just here in Britain, but in all advanced societies. In part this bigness arises from the imperfections and failures of the market in certain areas – for instance, where there is an inherent monopoly; partly it reflects public dissatisfaction with the inequalities of income which are generated by the free play of market forces; partly too it is an acknowledgment of the fact that some services, like defence, simply cannot be marketed. No matter how reverently the modern descendants of Locke and Smith treat the market, they accept that it cannot alone look after all our needs. In this country today the goods, services and transfers which the government commands are equivalent to more than 40 per cent of the national product; and all this with a government which has expressed a clear preference for relying on the market and the private sector wherever possible.

But in taking such a large part of the provision of our daily wants out of the market we have lost the in-built features that markets display at their best – efficiency and responsiveness. If the government and not the market provides us with health care, a prison service and so on, how can we as citizens be sure that it does so efficiently and in ways we collectively approve of? There are those who argue that in a parliamentary democracy my questions are easily answered: through the ballot box. Governments which are inefficient or unresponsive will sooner or later meet their fate at the hands of the electorate. But this is a simplistic view. It takes no account of the restricted choice which is presented to voters at general elections, nor of the limited information which is available to them when it comes to

6

expressing a choice. Useful, and indeed vital, as the electoral process is as a public sanction on our leaders, it is far from sufficient to guarantee the delivery of what I have set out as the prime requirements of government. I believe there is a pressing need for us as citizens to keep the daily conduct of government business under regular review, and to ask ourselves all the time whether it is being carried out in ways which satisfy us, and which give us, in the widest sense, value for money. It is after all our money that is being spent.

And this brings me to the task I have set myself in these lectures. Over the next six weeks I shall be seeking to examine how effectively in Britain today central government is equipped to secure these twin objectives of efficiency and responsiveness. I shall not be discussing the policies of governments or the objectives they have set, important as these are to the development of our society and to its well-being. Nor will I be reviewing the relationship between central and local government, even though this has now become an issue of great concern to us all and bears critically on the question of responsiveness. I do not intend to comment either on the system by which we elect our representatives, though this too is an important aspect of popular participation in policy-making. What I shall be doing is to look at the way our executive government is organised, at the mechanisms it uses to formulate its policies and the adequacy of the system by which it evaluates progress towards its objectives. I shall be looking at the machinery through which it is called to account. I shall ask what more it could do to promote public debate and understanding of issues of popular concern. And finally I shall be considering whether our system gives the ordinary citizen sufficient voice in the government of the country. My choice of subject inevitably reflects my own personal experience in government – a different experience would yield a different perspective.

In its most evident form, the problem of providing an efficient system of government arises in the day-to-day execution of administrative tasks: maintaining the services of law and order, paying welfare benefits and so on. It is here that huge sums of money are spent: something like one-fifth of government expenditure goes on administration. The efficiency of public administration has exercised governments for over a hundred years. Its central importance has been vigorously emphasised by the present government, whose efforts to reduce its cost and improve its effectiveness can only be applauded. But the search for efficiency in public administration is not a simple task. First of all, there is the problem of measurement. Much of the public service – because it is supplied free or substantially below cost – is not susceptible to the test of profit. The private sector, certainly if it is operating in a competitive environment, can gauge its efficiency by its profit performance. Although the output of government is something successive administrations have tried to measure, it has eluded capture except in some small areas. So judgments about efficiency in government become very subjective. Of course, if a given standard of service can be supplied by new techniques at lower cost, efficiency is improved. But most reductions in costs – the saving of staff, for instance – involve some deterioration of service, some exposure to fraud or loss, or – and this is something which is not always realised – some increase in cost to the people for whom the service is provided. Putting personal taxation on a self-assessment basis would not necessarily be an efficient step if the taxpayer had to expend more effort making his return than the Inland Revenue did when making the assessment for him. We would have reduced the number of civil servants, but we would not be a more efficient society. However, difficulties like this must not stand in the way of a continuing effort both to judge the efficacy of administration, and to improve it.

But if efficiency is an elusive concept to translate to the administration of individual departments, how much more difficult it is at the level of government policy as a whole. Even if each individual department is operating at peak efficiency, how can we be sure that the balance of effort between departments is right? I ask this question because the functions that government undertakes are both wide-ranging and disparate, far more so than those performed by any other entity in our society. When a business firm, even a conglomerate, has to decide which activities to pursue it can reduce its options to a common form, to the rate of return on assets, for instance, and an efficient decision becomes possible. But governments are not only undertaking widely divergent functions, ranging, for example, from immigration control to the provision of advice to exporters, but judgments about the amount of effort to put into each service cannot be founded on any standard or uniform basis of comparison, so difficult is it to compare the contribution each makes to the social good.

Before I come to the conceptual difficulties which complicate the making of choices between such unrelated and incommensurable issues as those I have instanced, it is worth looking at the conventions which apply to collective decisions. Governments, here as elsewhere, are organised on a functional basis, each department being headed by a minister whose personal responsibilities are usually defined by statute. But overriding almost all the individual responsibilities of ministers and departments runs the doctrine of the collective responsibility of the Cabinet. The Cabinet, some would say in formal terms, though I would say in real terms as well, is the ultimate embodiment of the executive government in this country. A minister may have statutory responsibilities peculiar to himself, but if the exercise of those responsibilities affects his colleagues, if, for example, he exposes the whole government to criticism and attack, or if he imposes costs on his fellow ministers, he must expect to submit his decision to collective endorsement.

The way issues are presented to Cabinet, indeed, the way issues are settled between departments, is crucially affected not only by these conventions, but also by the organisation of government. An issue which is brought to Cabinet for approval or resolution is always presented by the minister whose business it is. If it impinges other than tangentially on another minister he too may make a presentation to Cabinet, supporting or opposing the case of the minister who is principally concerned. But the essence of any collective Cabinet discussion is that it takes place on the basis of statements by interested

10

parties, and they can always be relied on to do their best by argument and presentation to secure approval for what they want to do. Where the proposals are contested by a colleague whose departmental interests are adversely affected, the discussion assumes an adversarial character and the Cabinet acts in what amounts to a judicial role. But where as so often happens, there is no adversary, the Cabinet simply hears the case which the minister concerned presents, and this case is inevitably put in terms which suit the minister himself.

Now it may be that in ideal circumstances the minister will present the issue with the same objectivity that his own officials have employed in presenting it to him. The Cabinet will then, as a minimum, have the same information as the minister, and its decision can be presumed to be an efficient one. But if for any reason the minister does not present all the relevant information to his colleagues, how then can the Cabinet be said to be taking an efficient decision?

In no area of policy-making does this problem arise more acutely than in the management of the economy and, in particular, the Budget. The minister who brings these issues to Cabinet is of course the Chancellor of the Exchequer. No other minister has at his command the back-up of analytical support that the Chancellor receives from his Treasury and Revenue Department officials and from the Bank of England. How can his colleagues be assured that they are getting the whole story and not just the one which the Chancellor wishes them to hear? They have no independent staff. They have indeed no direct access to the official advice which the

Treasury provides. Yet they are obliged to come to a view on the basis of what one of their colleagues, a committed party, is telling them. And they will be expected to defend that view in public as though it had been reached on the basis of full information.

The situation is perhaps not quite as sharply in conflict with the constitutional proprieties as it used to be. When I joined the Treasury just after the War, and indeed for many years afterwards, the Cabinet was not even invited to consider, let alone to have a voice in the making of the Budget. Although the Prime Minister was usually consulted beforehand, the most important aspect of economic policy was settled as a personal matter by the Chancellor of the day, and presented to his colleagues as a *fait accompli*. It was a matter of astonishment to me that successive Cabinets should have acquiesced in this procedure, given that the doctrine of collective responsibility obliged them to defend the Budget statement and, what is more, to live with its consequences. Today things are somewhat better, but the Cabinet as a whole remains at a disadvantage *vis-à-vis* the Chancellor, who keeps his powerful control of the sources of official information and advice. It is this feature of our system which makes it desirable that ministers collectively should have an alternative appraisal, on important issues at any rate, to the one provided by their colleague, a theme I shall be returning to in next week's lecture.

But if these are some of the problems which confront ministers collectively in making decisions on individual issues, how much more acute are they when they are considering a mass of different issues, which is the task they face when they are settling

12

public expenditure programmes. This task is argu-
ably the most important function which Cabinets
nowadays engage in, for although some activities of
government can still be performed costlessly, most of
its business cannot be carried out without spending a
lot of money. The control and allocation of public
expenditure is therefore a matter of crucial importance to ministers, and it must be in their and the
country's interest that the function is carried out
rationally and efficiently.

Over the past twenty years or so, governments
have steadily developed techniques to help them in
the rational determination of the total claims which
the public sector should make on the economy. The
Treasury makes regular forecasts of the likely trend
of the national product and is thereby able to offer
ministers different scenarios for taxation, personal
income, inflation and so on, on the basis of different
forward projections of the total of public spending.

These scenarios go a long way towards giving
ministers collectively enough material to make a
rational choice about the division of resources
between the public and the private sectors. Whether
they would prefer lower taxation to a higher level of
public services is, of course, a political decision and
different governments will have different views on
this. What is important is that ministers should take
their decision in possession of the relevant facts and
estimates and not on the basis of blind prejudice.

It is, however, when it comes to dividing the
agreed total between the various, different programmes that the concept of rationality begins to
come under strain. Decisions in this area are
governed by two well-entrenched, if rather arbitrary,

13

principles. Number one: 'as things have been, so broadly shall they remain'; and number two: 'he who has the muscle gets the money.' Let me explain what I mean. Principle number one stems from the Annual Public Expenditure Survey when departments make bids for future allocations of money on the basis of their existing plans and programmes. The implicit assumption is that these plans are 'right', in the sense that they were accepted in the past and that the only question is how rapidly or how slowly they should develop. Principle number two manifests itself in the process by which the individual bids for expenditure are settled. The essence of this process, given that the aggregate of bids invariably exceeds the agreed total, is that Treasury ministers have to do battle with all the spending ministers in turn. And the outcome of each battle is determined less by rational argument than by a judgment each party makes of the way the Cabinet would adjudicate in the event of continuing hostilities between the parties. Sometimes the Treasury will yield, knowing that the spending minister has a strong political case. Sometimes it is the minister who concedes, by not pressing his bid, perhaps through lack of conviction in the strength of his case. Unresolved conflicts are finally settled in full Cabinet.

Now there are a number of criticisms which can be made of this system, but first a word in its defence. The principle that programmes should develop much as they have in the past is not simply evidence of inertia on Whitehall's part. It is a reflection of political reality – the reality that in a pluralist society significant shifts in policies and programmes are liable to encounter strong opposi-

14

tion. And the principle of settling differences between the Treasury and the spenders on the basis of political strength, while crude and pragmatic, may well lead to a series of decisions which somehow reflect rational choice. A spending minister who lacks conviction in his programme may be expressing the implicit view of his colleagues and his party. If he concedes readily to the Treasury, he may be doing so not out of weakness but in recognition that his programme does not command high priority. He may feel he can deal with the beneficiaries of his spending programme more easily than his colleagues can with theirs, and this in turn may reflect the political strength of the interest groups affected. So at the end of the day the distribution may take quite a lot of account, albeit implicitly, of political preferences.

But it is clearly not a very scientific process, and most theorists of collective decision-taking would find it unsatisfactory. Now the system could be made a bit more rational and efficient if it incorporated some feature for giving ministers a 'feel' for the relative value to them of different parts of their whole programme. I mentioned earlier the difficulty of comparing the value of the immigration service and the provision of advice to exporters. Let no-one imagine that such comparisons are easy. But I believe that more could be done by sophisticated cost-benefit analysis to give ministers a sounder basis than they have at present for exercising choice about where to expand and where to contract government services, and to help them away from the inefficient and indiscriminate approach where cuts have to be made uniformly and across the board. Another feature I would like to see would be one for regularly evaluating the expenditure incurred on each programme against the objectives it was designed to achieve. The world is a changing place: administrative techniques, social habits, industrial performance and so on are not static, and government programmes should respond flexibly to changes like this in the environment. I do not doubt that many government departments do periodically ask themselves whether an entire programme should be redesigned to reflect changing circumstances. But the system as it operates today does not encourage this. It is far easier to get the Treasury and the Cabinet to agree to unchanged programmes than to persuade them that programmes should be modified as circumstances change, especially if the variations involve temporary increases in expenditure. The Treasury's proper concern to limit the total claims of the public sector sometimes leads it to resist any increase in programmes, whatever the benefits may be in terms of improved efficiency.

It would be possible to counter these 'inertial' features of the present system by making two specific changes. The first would be to make the spending departments think what they would do if the money available to them were drastically cut. Just as the ordinary person or the ordinary business has, from time to time, to face a sharp reduction in income, so departments would have to think, either of different, cheaper, ways of realising their objectives or of scrapping some objectives altogether. This system, which is known in the jargon as zero-based budgeting, has often been considered in the past. But it has always been rejected, either because the programme managers have convinced themselves that alternative ways of carrying out their policies were simply not available, or because ministers were not prepared to abandon some aims altogether. These are under-standable reactions, but the arguments against change do not really convince me. I would therefore like to see zero-based budgeting tried out, in the first place on a selective basis, to see whether it is as unworkable as the spenders have always argued in the past.

The second change, which would have something like the same effect, would be to reinstate a regime which Mr Heath's administration introduced over ten years ago, the regime of policy analysis and review, 'PAR' for short. This system required Whitehall to comb over its programmes and find out whether they were working in the way they had been intended to. Take transport, for instance. The idea of 'PAR' would be to mount a searching review of the government's various policies towards public and private transport, to see whether they were contributing to the creation of a coherent system of roads, railways, canals, airports and so on, which matched the users' requirements. The instruments used to bring about these policy aims, for instance the taxation of cars, investment spending on the railways, the licensing of civil air routes and so on, would be examined to see how effective they were, and if the policies were not producing the desired results, they would become candidates for change. The concept was admirable, but in practice it did not come off. Why not? In part the answer is that each 'PAR' imposed a heavy burden on officials and many of the reviews led to no perceptible change in policy.

The effort seemed pointless. The cost of each radical review was the neglect of some part of the continuing job of administration. But another reason why the system fell into disuse was that many departments chose to offer relatively unimportant programmes for analysis and kept their major policies out of the area of review.

The experience of the 1970s should give anyone pause before recommending the reinstatement of 'PAR'. But I believe its demise was not due to any inherent flaw or defect and a new generation of officials, and a firm commitment by ministers, could make it a success. The effort it would involve could be amply repaid by the substantial rewards to be gained in even a few programmes. The Treasury has made a start in this direction by calling for departmental reviews at the conclusion of each annual expenditure survey. This needs to be given strong ministerial support.

This brings me to my last point and it is one which inevitably arises from the concept of review and reappraisal of policy. To what extent should governments be prepared to adapt policy to changing circumstances? A policy which governments cling to long after the evidence has shown it is not doing what it was meant to do is plainly inefficient. All governments face this problem from time to time, because policies rarely produce their desired results quickly. Steadfastness of policy in the face of adversity and setbacks is a desirable quality in governments as it is in other organisations. Plutarch wrote wisely when he said that 'to be turned from one's course by men's opinions, by blame and by misrepresentation, shows a man unfit to hold office.'

But steadfastness or inflexibility in the teeth of clear evidence of policy failure is another matter. The word 'pragmatism' has acquired a certain stigma: it is interpreted to mean a willingness to change course at the first reverse. But governments must be pragmatic. In the science of politics we know very little *a priori* about the likely results of a radical policy development. Given this ignorance, it is surely right that policies should be rigorously evaluated and their effects set against their objectives. Dependent as they are for political support on a public perception of their competence and resolve, it may be hard for governments to admit that they have been wrong. But without the strength of moral purpose to make such an admission they may in the long run expose themselves and the country to risks and dangers which far exceed the costs of a policy change.

I find it difficult to believe that, starkly as he saw the contrast between good and bad government, Lorenzetti would not have expected his benign prince to apply his ruling hand in a flexible and responsive way.

LECTURE 2

Cabinet: Directorate or Directory?

Anyone who has had the privilege of mingling with the assembly of Cabinet ministers as they wait outside the Cabinet room at No. 10 could be forgiven for mistaking it for the preliminary to a Sunday school outing. These twenty or so men and women bear with equanimity, even lightheartedness, the formidable task which lies ahead: the resolution of weighty issues which will affect, perhaps change, the lives of their fellow citizens. But once Cabinet begins, it is all quite different – or at least it is all said to be different, because I am speaking from hearsay, as I have never assisted my minister at a Cabinet meeting. The highest organ of executive government meets very privately, usually once a week, for two or three hours. A summary of its discussion is circulated the day after the meeting and Whitehall, or that part of it which is now allowed to see the record, eagerly scrutinises its marching orders.

But the term 'marching orders' is a misnomer. Cabinet does not behave like a high command issuing orders to its field officers. And Cabinet minutes rarely tell the reader what the strategy of the government is, still less how the strategy is to be prosecuted. Military men who go into politics must find the workings of government even more frustrating than businessmen do.

Every organisation needs a central directing authority, and in the British system of government the doctrine of collective responsibility places the Cabinet in that role. But how well does it do its job? Is the Cabinet an efficient body? Could it be made more effective? These are the questions I shall be trying to answer this week.

But let me start with the composition of the Cabinet. Each departmental minister is an individual with specific functions usually defined by statute. He has an experienced department at his service, able both to advise him on the ordering of his priorities and to despatch work in accordance with his directions. He and his department are closely in touch with the groups whose special interests are affected by his responsibilities. And while, as I shall argue, he may in his decision-taking not always incline himself as much as I would wish to long-term and structural issues, on his own ground each minister is an impressive force, almost irrespective of his personal qualities.

But when he comes together with his colleagues in Cabinet things assume a different form. The machinery which exists within departments to give ministers a perspective of all their activities, a set of suggested objectives and a ranking of priorities, is missing in the collective forum of the Cabinet. Ministers in Cabinet rarely look at the totality of their responsibilities, at the balance of policy, at the progress of the government towards its objectives as a whole. Apart from its ritual weekly review of foreign affairs and parliamentary business, Cabinet's staple diet consists of a selection of individually important one-off cases or of issues on which the ministers departmentally concerned are unable to agree.

The form and structure of a modern Cabinet and the diet it consumes almost oblige it to function like a group of individuals, and not as a unity. Indeed for each minister, the test of his success in office lies in his ability to deliver his departmental goals. Mr Macmillan's 300,000 houses provided him with the initial success which eventually took him to No. 10. No minister I know of has won political distinction by his performance in Cabinet or by his contribution to collective decision-taking. To the country and the House of Commons he is simply the minister for such-and-such a department and the only member of the Cabinet who is not seen in this way is the Prime Minister.

None of this is new. Richard Crossman's diaries describe vividly how ministers participate in Cabinet as departmental champions. Lord Rothschild recalls how he once stole a glimpse of a minister's brief for Cabinet: the departmental officials who had drawn it up had thoughtfully marked one heading for discussion with the comment, 'This item is of no interest to you.' What a far cry this is from Rousseau's ideal of the general will being more than the summation of the special interests of individual groups!

The characteristics I have described carry with them two main consequences. The first consequence is that the general thrust of the government's policies is seldom if ever reviewed and assessed by Cabinet; strategic changes of course in response to substantial shifts in circumstances are not subjected to collective consideration; and the ordering of priorities is discussed in only the most general terms. I am not saying that these matters are never reviewed by governments: I can recall several important policy changes in the field of economic management which governments have made as the result of a deliberate reassessment. But they were not usually Cabinet reviews; and none of them was the result of a systematic study. The second consequence is that Cabinet does not have adequate safeguards against a strong departmental minister. An issue which comes to Cabinet is presented by the minister whose interests and reputation are involved, and he is bound to be partisan. No mechanism exists to enable the Cabinet to challenge his view unless the interests of another minister are involved, and even then the challenge itself may be partisan. Cabinet can too easily be railroaded.

It would be wrong to suggest that senior politicians have been blind to the defects of Cabinet government as we know it. Fifty years ago Leo Amery, himself an experienced minister, was writing that 'a Cabinet consisting of a score of overworked departmental Ministers is quite incapable of either thinking out a definite policy or of securing its effective and consistent execution.' In recent years several prime ministers have sought to engage the attention of their colleagues on matters of strategy, frequently setting aside a day at Chequers to emphasise the distinction between a wide-ranging review of policy and the day-to-day preoccupations of Downing Street. The idea is a good one, but its application has not led to any marked change in the collective

26

performance of Cabinets. Seminars too have been held on matters as general and strategic as the fight against inflation, the control of public expenditure, energy conservation and so on. But they have taken place at such a high level of generality and abstraction that they have rarely led to any discernible change when it came to particular cases. To be told simply that the Cabinet has decided to give high priority to fighting inflation or to the solution of the Rhodesian problem is not much help to the officials who have to translate aspirations into action.

I can think of two possible institutional changes which might help Cabinets to function more cohesively in their approach to policy as a whole. The first would be to bias the composition of the Cabinet away from the departmental minister. The second would be to supply the Cabinet with a staff whose job would be to identify the issues and choices which Cabinet must face as a collective entity. I want to look at these two ideas in turn.

One way to reduce the influence of the departmental minister would be to restructure the Cabinet completely and create a high-command on the model of the War Cabinets of 1916 and 1939. The Cabinet would be a small, closely-knit group of senior ministers, who would be mainly without departmental responsibilities: they would not therefore have any prior commitment on any issue by virtue of their office. Ministers in charge of departments would be outside the Cabinet and would come to it as supplicants to a higher body, not as equal members of it. It would be for departmental ministers to decide, as now, which issues required Cabinet approval and which did not. But once a

27

matter went to the Cabinet the departmental minister would have less of a voice in the decision than he has now. He might well find himself having to stomach decisions affecting his responsibilities with which he did not agree. And these he would have to defend in public.

The attractions of departmental office would diminish, but, by the same token, membership of the small 'inner' Cabinet would greatly enhance the authority and power of the individual concerned. Cabinet members would be largely free from the appalling administrative burdens to which departmental ministers are subject; the business of answering parliamentary questions, meetings with interest groups, representation at meetings abroad and so on. They would be able to concentrate upon policy in its broadest sense. What is more they would have time, as the present type of Cabinet does not, to think about the longer-term aspects of current issues.

A system like this has a lot of attractions. One of the most eloquent expressions of its virtues was given in a speech Lord Curzon made to the House of Lords in 1918, when he contrasted the effectiveness of the first War Cabinet at despatching business with that of the conventional Cabinet. The idea bears a family resemblance to a proposal made by the Plowden Committee, when it reviewed the control of public expenditure in 1961. In that instance, the idea was to strengthen the hand of the Chancellor of the Exchequer by creating a Committee of Cabinet ministers, mainly without portfolios, to determine the level of all the departmental spending programmes. Here, too, spending ministers were to come as supplicants and not as full members. Several attempts have been made in the past twenty-five years to implement this proposal, and the Treasury has nearly always supported them. But each attempt has ended abortively, mainly because no spending minister who was strongly opposed to the conclusions of the Cabinet Committee would relinquish his right of appeal to the full Cabinet, in which, of course, he was a full member and where he could expect a more sympathetic hearing. The inner Cabinet idea is free from the defect of appeal, as its decisions would be final.

Nevertheless there are powerful objections to it. Churchill himself was reluctant to have his War Cabinet composed entirely of non-departmental ministers, and he expressed the view that they 'tend to become more and more theoretical supervisors and commentators, reading an immense amount of material every day, but doubtful how to use their knowledge without doing more harm than good'.

I sympathise with this view. In my experience of administration I have found it almost impossible to think constructively about general policy issues if I have not been involved in particular practical cases. I have often discussed with my fellow civil servants the question of how to give more attention to longer-term problems. We have considered, as indeed the Fulton Report recommended, whether the task of strategic thinking could be given to planning units who would be free from the cares of day-to-day administration. But we have usually concluded that only by being involved in everyday issues can people identify the longer-term general problems and construct suitable solutions.

Even more worrying, I see a real possibility that

with a Cabinet of eight or so ministers without portfolio, individual members would tend to become specialists in certain areas. One minister might focus on foreign policy, one on social policy, and so on. The departmental minister would then identify the relevant Cabinet member whose ear it was most worth his while to catch. He would be invited to departmental presentations, and supplied with personal departmental briefing, all to get him on the department's side. Gradually what might emerge would be a collection of super-departmental ministers rather like the Overlords which Churchill devised in his peacetime administration in 1951. That was not by any means a success. It may be that in time of war, when there is a single, overriding aim to be pursued, the idea is viable. But I am driven to the conclusion, reluctantly, that in peacetime, when the government has many different objectives, the inner Cabinet concept would not be a satisfactory solution to the problem I have identified.

Another, less radical approach to Cabinet reform might be to develop our system of Cabinet committees. New committees would be set up to review specific issues like housing, the social services, transport, the functioning of the nationalised industries and so on. They could accommodate the ministers directly involved, together with a number who had no relevant departmental responsibilities. Their composition would enable them not only to oversee a whole field of policy, but also to ensure that the ministers functionally involved were not carried away by their departments and lobbies. But it would also be their job to relate the policy area within their purview to the government's broader political objectives.

Cabinet committees have not in the past functioned as review bodies or strategic commands, though the word 'strategy', whether hopefully or misleadingly, has sometimes been incorporated in their title. Most of them have been preoccupied with the kind of case-work where there has been a regular need for inter-departmental consultation and coordination. When the government of the day has had a prices and incomes policy, for instance, a Cabinet committee has been set up to clear individual problems and to ensure consistency of application by all departments. It is true that committees have been established as a one-off measure to review particular policies and to produce a report, but this has been more common at the official than at the ministerial level. I cannot recall any government systematically establishing Cabinet committees with the purposes and aims I have described.

It would be a fair question to ask whether I would have liked to see such a committee operating in the field of financial and economic policy while I was at the Treasury. The honest answer has to be that I would have found it a great nuisance, and I am sure the Chancellors I have served would have done too. But I have to concede that it would have been an excellent discipline for the Treasury and that only good could have come from the independent scrutiny of our assumptions and doctrines; and it would have done much to give non-Treasury ministers a greater sense of participation in the management of the economy.

While each review committee might be able to coordinate the various facets of the policy for which it was responsible and to oversee the work of the relevant departments, a network of them would not necessarily help in the integration of government policy as a whole. No body below the level of Cabinet can do that. But I do believe that the idea of Cabinet review committees having standing remits and obliged, as I hope they would be, to produce an annual report for Cabinet, would do quite a lot to make the Cabinet into a more corporate body.

There is of course a school, of which Mr Crossman was a member, which argues that we should frankly acknowledge that the British Cabinet as we know it is not able to act like a high command. This school would like to develop still further the notion that the Prime Minister is the only person in charge of government policy as a whole, and hence the only person who can determine priorities. To realise this concept in full, the Prime Minister would need a department of advisers in much the same way that the American President has his army of personal staff in the executive offices of the White House.

But giving the Prime Minister the responsibility and the means to co-ordinate policy, to order priorities and to challenge in detail the proposals of individual departments, would be very difficult to reconcile with the principle of collective responsibility as we know it. We would be taking a significant step towards a presidential form of government, with a single chief executive advised and assisted by departmental chiefs. The Prime Minister would have the power to impose his will on the Cabinet in a way that we have never known, even in war. The Cabinet would begin to resemble the American Cabinet, which is little more than a consultative body for the President.

Those who would like to see the Prime Minister assume greater responsibilities argue that he is already in a dominating position. He alone has the power to appoint and dismiss ministers, and to control the composition of Cabinet committees. He it is who decides what may or may not go on the Cabinet agenda, and when to go to the country. Moreover the Prime Minister has come to expect to be consulted, personally and outside the Cabinet, by departmental ministers when they are contemplating important steps within their own competence. For instance, every Chancellor I have worked for has obtained the Prime Minister's agreement to changes, even quite trivial ones, in the way the economy is run. The pure doctrine of collective responsibility should surely have required the Chancellor to consult the Cabinet as a whole if he felt he needed backing, but this he did not do.

On top of this, economic summits, European Council meetings, Prime Minister's Question Time and so on, have all led to a much greater involvement of the Prime Minister in what used to be purely departmental affairs. Finally, our general elections have assumed something of the character of presidential contests.

In spite of these developments, I believe the Cabinet remains the supreme governing body and I believe it is right that it should be. Prime ministers are not, like presidents, elected by direct popular suffrage. Indeed, within the past thirty years four of our seven prime ministers have taken office without having won a general election. More importantly, the fact that the power to take decisions on major policy resides in the Cabinet, and not in the Prime Minister alone, has provided us with a valuable constitutional check. Prime ministers have to take account of Cabinet revolts and Cabinet opposition. Cabinet represents a cross-section of the majority party, and its decisions in my view are more likely to command parliamentary support than decisions of the Prime Minister alone. For these reasons, I would not favour any further strengthening of the Prime Minister's position in relation to his colleagues.

All this suggests that despite the weaknesses of Cabinet as a collective entity, there are no easy institutional alternatives to what we have at present. But before I look at my second suggestion, I want to deal with an issue which has been widely canvassed over the last few years: the idea that the Prime Minister, within the present structure of Cabinet government and by virtue of the role he has already acquired, should have a staff of his own. Without such a staff, so the argument goes, the Prime Minister is at the mercy of the departmental minister and his advisers, and will rapidly become the creature of the departmental brief.

I have never been persuaded by this argument. As the Prime Minister has been drawn into departmental business he has found it possible to call directly on the services of the official advisers in the departments concerned. During the past dozen years or so many officials, some of them quite junior, have become familiar with the inside of No. 10, having been summoned to give personal briefing on issues with which the Prime Minister has become involved.

While, of course, these advisers owe their first

allegiance to their departmental minister, they would never withhold help or information from the Prime Minister. I would not deny that where a departmental minister was pursuing a policy of which the Prime Minister was only a lukewarm supporter, he might be reluctant to see his officials supplying information which did not support his line; and in theory he could instruct his officials not to communicate directly with No. 10. But if this unhappy situation did emerge it would be an indication of a fundamentally unhealthy situation in Cabinet, which should really be resolved by other means than the creation of a Prime Minister's department.

So if my thoughts lead me to the conclusion that, with the possible exception of Cabinet review committees, we are unlikely to promote strategic decision-taking by reforming the system of government, where is it that we should be looking for improvement? I think the answer lies in some strengthening of the staff which serves the Cabinet as a whole.

As government is now organised, the Cabinet as a body has at its own service only the Cabinet Secretariat. This is a tiny staff, headed by the Cabinet Secretary, and its job is to prepare the agendas and compile the minutes of meetings of both Cabinet and the Cabinet committees. It also briefs the various chairmen of the Cabinet and its committees, but it does so mainly, if not indeed entirely, on procedural matters. Where a clearly exposed conflict has emerged, it may suggest a possible compromise to the chairman. But its advice is privy to the chairman and it is not available to the Cabinet or to the Cabinet committee as a whole.

Clearly this is not the body I have in mind to strengthen the directing capability of Cabinet. Something of what we need is to be found in the role originally seen for the Central Policy Review Staff — known in Whitehall, with its affection for initials, as the CPRS and to the wider public, more graphically, as the Think Tank.

When the CPRS was set up in 1970, a White Paper was issued defining its functions. The main task seen for it was to work out the implications of the government's basic strategy in terms of particular policies. For instance, if the government set the defeat of inflation as a strategic objective, the Review Staff would be expected to say what contribution could be made to this aim from such areas as public sector pricing, indirect taxation, the exchange rate, public borrowing and so on. The idea was to produce a well-orchestrated and co-ordinated attack on the problem, and not to set about it in piecemeal fashion. Another function the architects of the CPRS had in mind was that it would suggest relative priorities for different parts of the government's programme. It would offer views, for instance, on whether more resources should be put into industrial policy and fewer into social policy. Another task would be to identify those areas of policy where a completely new approach might be made: the unthinkable, by implication, was not to be excluded. Finally, it was thought that the CPRS might be the instrument for ensuring that, when ministers looked at new policy options, all the implications of each option would be brought to the surface. If ministers were thinking of some shift in our external trade policy, for instance, the CPRS might be expected to examine the effect of this shift on industry and employment in the different regions, on consumer prices, on foreign policy and so on.

The CPRS had a chequered history and it was abolished earlier this year. These two facts ought to make anyone hesitate before proposing to resurrect it. At the very least we have to ask why it did not give satisfaction to its ministerial chiefs. There are many reasons for this. In the first place, the role it was given was too ambitious. I do not believe a small central staff by itself can be expected to identify new areas of workable policy which have somehow escaped the attention of the expert department. Nor can it really evaluate the implications of alternative courses: that, too, is best left to the specialists. What the Think Tank should have concentrated on was what I have called 'the balance of policy', in other words the way the government's programmes fitted into its strategic objectives, and the way it ordered its priorities. It should also have taken more seriously the job of criticising departmental proposals where it had evidence that they had unperceived implications for other parts of the programme.

The CPRS never had enough staff to perform even these more limited tasks. Its first chief insisted on keeping its size down to the level at which all the members could sit round his personal conference table. A central analytical staff which is to carry out more than superficial appraisals of policy must be prepared to do a lot of detailed work, on a continuing basis and in a wide variety of areas, if it is to make any worthwhile judgments about the whole. It must have the time and capacity to master the intricacies of a good deal of government activity, in the same sort of way that the Treasury expenditure divisions do. In the Treasury, there are about four times as many people engaged in this 'marking' role as there were in the CPRS, and this provides a measure of the relative depth in which each organisation was able to tackle any problem. But despite its small size, the CPRS embarked on many studies which were plainly not its job. Its examination of the car industry was something that should have been done by the Department of Industry, and its review of Britain's overseas representation could well have been done by the Civil Service Department. As time went by, it concerned itself less and less with central issues and became a meddler in departmental business. The decision to abolish it was a not unjustified recognition that it had lost its way and no longer filled the role intended for it. But one reason why the CPRS was not able to provide the Cabinet with the service which its architects had envisaged was that it was only rarely engaged in the day-to-day business of government at the working level. Its activities were episodic, a foray here and a foray there. And not being continuously involved, as the Treasury has to be, in all the various and important parts of the government's programme it was unable to comment authoritatively on the whole.

But if the Central Policy Review Staff failed to realise the hopes that were originally placed in it, must we infer that all attempts to create a body which can serve the Cabinet as a whole and supply it with strategic appraisals are doomed? I do not think we have to be quite so pessimistic.

To avoid a repetition of the failure and disappointment of the CPRS, I believe that a newly established central analytical staff would need to be given new guidelines and safeguards. It should be given the resources needed for what would be a demanding role, a role which, as I have hinted, would draw it into Whitehall's day-to-day business. Fortunately, the record of departmental co-operation with the old CPRS was good. But to make absolutely sure that the Review Staff was in touch with departmental business, it would have to be closely involved in the annual public expenditure survey and it should be represented at all the bilateral meetings between the Treasury and the spending ministers, not least to ensure that the Cabinet had, in effect, a watching brief over any private deals which might be struck.

I would also want it to produce its own report as the survey proceeded and to suggest its own solutions to the problems of choice which the survey invariably presents, and which I referred to in my first lecture. To those who would argue that I would be creating a duplication of effort at the centre of government, I reply that this would be a small price to pay for a more effective centre.

But another feature of the staff that I think would be essential is that it should be free-standing in the structure of Whitehall. It should be the servant of the Cabinet as a whole and should not become, as the CPRS did, the creature of the Prime Minister alone. Indeed it is arguable that the sidetracking of the CPRS into specialist areas like industry was due to pressure from No. 10, rather than a result of its own work programme.

With these safeguards and with encouragement from the Cabinet as a whole to offer bold and provocative advice about the balance of policy, a unit like this would force ministers in their collective embodiment to realise that they have to make choices and that by facing the issues which those choices impose, they stand only to gain. If we persist in ignoring the need of our political masters for the help which a review staff could provide we shall be choosing, in our typically British way, to go on muddling through.

LECTURE 3

The Privileged Adviser

In the competition I took in 1946 to enter the Civil Service, the candidates were asked to give their reasons for applying. Most of us gave fairly conventional answers, but one, perhaps a little less orthodox with his background in the commandos, said quite simply 'to stop the worst excesses of the Labour Government'. The constitutional niceties of this remark, and − taking a rather wider canvas − the role of the Civil Service in helping to deliver efficient and responsive government, are the questions I shall be considering in this lecture.

Whatever the form it has taken, the Civil Service has played for a long time a key part in the government of this country. It existed long before we had any politicians, at least as we understand the term today. What distinguishes a civil servant from a politician is not only the degree of his involvement in the political process, the struggle for power and office; but, equally important, the degree of public responsibility he must accept for the acts of government. Though we now try to draw a sharp distinction in this country between the politician and the civil servant, the dividing line can easily become blurred. In some countries, notably the United

States, the senior civil servant has many of the attributes of a politician and vice versa.

For the past hundred years or so, we have sought in this country to sharpen the separation of the official from the politician by requiring of the official two qualities: political neutrality and recruitment on the strict basis of merit. The aptness of this was argued in the Northcote/Trevelyan Report of 1854, a report which had been prompted by public disquiet over the inefficiencies of the government in its handling of the Crimean War. Political patronage had led to nepotism and to the use of the Civil Service as a source of sinecures for those to whom ministers had some personal obligation. The motive for the reform was the promotion of efficiency, and efficiency was thought to be best secured by taking the politics out of administration. Between 1870, when the Northcote/Trevelyan reforms were fully implemented, and the beginning of the Second World War, the principle of a politically neutral, career Civil Service went unchallenged. The improvement in the quality of the administration over what had preceded the reforms was plainly visible, and most observers accepted that Britain had the best Civil Service in the world.

Today that judgment is challenged. 'Taking the politics out of administration' is seen by some critics as a veiled means of ensuring that the values and attitudes of a permanent high Civil Service are insidiously imposed on the ministers it serves. The continuity of tenure of office creates a presumption of continuity of policy. And a reforming government, which by virtue of its election to office must be presumed to reflect the public mood, will be frustrated – so the argument goes – by the cleverness, the conservatism, and the lack of public sensitivity of its official advisers. We all enjoy Sir Humphrey Appleby's cynical manipulation of Jim Hacker. But how many of us believe it to be a portrait, perhaps a little exaggerated, of reality? And I wonder too how many of us, half believing it to be true, are secretly a little bit pleased that it is?

The line which separates the politically committed and publicly responsible minister from the politically neutral permanent official is drawn at a particularly high level in Britain. In practically no other country is there so little change in the administrative apparatus when a new government takes office. Officials who advise in favour of a particular policy, and devise means of implementing it, cheerfully accept the same responsibilities in regard to the diametrically opposite policy when the government of the day changes. Foreigners find this incomprehensible and wonder how our civil servants can retain the commitment and the dedication they need to do their job in the face of such sharp political shifts in direction. And many of our own citizens ask whether senior civil servants are not all modern equivalents of the Vicar of Bray.

In our system, the central government machine of over 600,000 people has at the top only a hundred or so politically appointed ministers and special advisers. The rest are permanent officials. Of course, the great majority of these have jobs which call for no political judgment: paying social security benefits, collecting taxes, servicing the armed forces and so on. But the senior ranks of the administration group, numbering about 3,000, are operating every day in the field of public policy: working closely with ministers, advising on delicate political matters and identifying initiatives to be examined and followed.

The presumption on which the system operates is that the Civil Service is unswervingly dedicated to the democratic parliamentary process and to the paramountcy of ministers in decision-taking. The professional ethic it has embraced requires it to give unqualified loyalty to its departmental ministers and to seek to the best of its ability to put the government's policies into execution. In advising ministers it should take their political objectives as given and regard it as its duty to secure those objectives in the most efficient and publicly acceptable way. This apparently rigorous definition of its role, however, begs a number of questions.

Where for instance do political objectives end and administrative methods begin? The definition I have given neatly presupposes that ministers define their objectives and officials devise ways of implementing them. In practice, that distinction of function is frequently blurred. Ministers do not always define their political objectives or if they do, they define them in terms which permit quite a lot of discretion in their interpretation. On the other hand, administrative methods are often highly charged political issues. The way a tax is administered may greatly affect the political standing of the government; and the use of some administrative techniques may be anathema to ministers. So in the real world ministers and civil servants are inextricably mixed up with each other. And they can only function on the basis of a close and harmonious partnership in which each has the trust of the other.

In recent years this trust has not always been taken for granted. Richard Crossman was perhaps the first politician to express misgivings about the subordination of civil servants to their political chiefs. Running through his diaries there is a suspicion that civil servants are seeking all the time to substitute their own value judgments and their own policy preferences for those of their ministers; and that because they are more familiar than politicians with the machinery of Whitehall, and because they have – or so it would seem – a common perception of what is desirable, they are able to out-manoeuvre ministers at the political game. As an instance of how this is done, Mr Crossman cites the existence of a network of Whitehall relationships at official level which cuts across departmental boundaries and leads to the formulation of a Whitehall view which is accepted by all senior officials whatever department they are in. This view is then presented to each departmental minister in a quite disingenuous way, as though it had emerged from the departmental machine as a straightforward attempt to further the minister's interests.

Some support for this view was thought to be given by the unauthorised disclosure, in early 1979, of confidential correspondence I had been having with Sir Peter Carey, my opposite number in the Department of Industry. The correspondence was about the effect on the national economy of the substantial government help which was being given to what the Treasury regarded as uneconomic industrial projects. I had referred in my letter to the need 'to secure a higher rejection rate' of applications for assistance, and I had done so without reference to my minister. Here was a Whitehall conspiracy unmasked: the mandarins were secretly ganging up on the Cabinet! The reality however was less sensational.

I never had any expectation that Sir Peter Carey would surrender any part of his minister's position and this indeed proved to be the case. Even more important, my correspondence with him was only a skirmishing, a reconnaissance if you like, as a preliminary to my submitting the issue to my own minister to whom I was able to give a conspectus of the sort of opposition he would encounter from his colleagues if he decided to act on my advice. But leaving this incident aside, who is right: the theorist who argues that the official is the creature and servant of the minister, or the cynic who argues that Whitehall manoeuvres the politicians? The answer, in my view, is that the theorist is by far the closer to the truth. But he is not wholly right, for a number of reasons.

First there is the problem of ends and means to which I referred a moment ago. Given the balance between ministers and officials, roughly one hundred to three thousand, a great many decisions on the despatch of government business have to be taken by officials without reference to ministers. Officials will be guided by known ministerial attitudes and objectives, and a skilled civil servant will get a great deal of satisfaction from the correct reading of his minister's mind, even in ambiguous circumstances. I myself had to take a number of quite political decisions in 1976, when I represented the government at the meeting of the International Monetary Fund in Manila and began the process of negotiating the financial assistance we needed. Of course I reported back to my political chiefs on what I was doing, and I had anyway secured the necessary authority for the way I was to conduct the discussions with the Fund and with our other potential creditors. But the execution was mine and the objective I aimed at was to say what I thought Mr Healey would have said, had he been able to attend the conference. On other occasions I have had to act for my minister when I was far from clear what position he would have taken. At such moments I had to do what I thought was right and rely on the confidence that I felt my minister had in me. So we come back once more, to this all-important issue of trust between ministers and their advisers.

But, even granted a large measure of mutual trust, the senior official cannot always escape his own value judgments and preserve intact his neutrality on policy objectives. You will remember my saying that policy objectives are issues for ministerial choice and decision. They are at the heart of politics. But, true as that is, it is sometimes difficult for civil servants to stand back and not seek to influence decisions on those objectives. Long exposure to a problem may have led them to the conclusion that a certain policy course is in some sense 'right' for the country and that any other course is 'wrong'.

This amounts to what one of my predecessors, Lord Bridges, once described as the departmental view: an opinion about policy which is widely shared at official level throughout the whole department. It may be difficult for permanent officials to avoid coming to this sort of conclusion.

They are, after all, greatly experienced in policy analysis and evaluation. They are usually highly intelligent people with a strong sense of public service and a commitment to the long-term well-being of the country. These are commendable characteristics, but they carry with them the risk that the political sense of officials may be unduly sharpened and lead them to overstep the boundaries of their proper role. While most civil servants have no difficulty recognising the limits to their authority, many are confronted at some point in their careers with a minister who wishes to do something they consider to be thoroughly inefficient if not perverse. Now a good official will not normally take a single apparently perverse decision by his minister as the final word: he will seek to bring him round to his own way of thinking. Indeed, if his professional conscience drives him to argue for a course of action which – within the framework set by ministers – he believes to be right, it is positively his duty to face any unpopularity he may be courting. A wise minister will respect an official who does this, and realise that an apparently tiresome adviser may be the best safeguard against his own folly. I like to think that our Civil Service resembles the ancient Netherlands Order of the Golden Fleece, a company whose duty it was to give advice to the Dutch ruler and to be bound by solemn oath to speak freely, honestly and under privilege. But if he fails to persuade his minister on a particular issue, what should a civil servant do? As our system operates his duty is to accept, as phlegmatically as possible, the verdict of the publicly accountable minister. However, there are those who believe that the Civil

Service should, as they put it, 'fight for the policies it believes to be right'; and there has been some discussion as to whether a civil servant who feels strongly that his minister is doing the wrong thing in a particular matter, should not have some sanction or recourse.

Let me say at once that I do not believe there can be any justification for civil servants fighting for the policies they believe to be right by underhand means: by the sort of briefing of the press and of the Opposition which disgruntled members of the Armed Forces are alleged to have undertaken when their particular service was under threat. But what about the possibility of a more reputable means of appeal, involving perhaps some modification to our existing procedures? One such means would be to entitle a senior official who considers that his minister has acted perversely to make his position known to some parliamentary body.

The idea may seem quite novel, but it is worth recalling that under our system as it stands, a permanent secretary may dissociate himself from a decision where a minister has acted improperly or unlawfully in the matter of public expenditure. The permanent secretary (or the Accounting Officer, as he is known for this purpose) is required to take steps which will bring the matter to the attention of the Public Accounts Committee. If a senior civil servant also had the right – to be used of course only in extreme circumstances – to inform the appropriate parliamentary body of his strong dissent from the minister's policy decision on ground of efficiency, that could act as a brake on a perverse course of action by the minister.

This is a possibility which many officials, and indeed some commentators outside government, would like to see implemented. It would put senior officials in something like the position of the judiciary who can, if appealed to, review certain ministerial decisions where there has been irregularity in the procedure by which they have been reached. It is not however a mechanism that I think would work, and it would carry with it some serious objections. It would, for instance, give the unelected official more power than is warranted in a democratic system. The emergence in public of a strong difference between the minister and his principal adviser would be damaging to the minister's standing, particularly in Parliament, where the Opposition would make maximum political capital out of his embarrassment; and it would also be damaging to the sense of mutual loyalty which should inform the relationship between the minister and his advisers. For this reason it would give impetus to the case for placing the senior administrative posts of government in the hands of political nominees, who could be counted on not to rock the boat by publicly dissenting from some action by the minister.

But what is a career civil servant to do if he finds himself having to implement a policy with which he may strongly disagree? As I have already said, his professional code requires him to carry out his instructions with complete loyalty. But how enthusiastically and how energetically should he be expected to do this? Enthusiasm may be asking rather a lot, but I have my doubts, in any case, about its place in administration: it can colour judgment and lead to unwise decisions. Even the politically committed should be wary of enthusiasm. But energy is a different matter. This is a question of conscience, and of dedication to the professional ethic. The energetic pursuit of ministerial objectives is something that must be required of officials. And this obligation on civil servants transcends by far any qualms they feel about the rightness of policy.

Pushed to extremes, of course, this sounds like the philosophy of Eichmann and of the German officials who loyally carried out the orders of the Hitler regime on the grounds that it was not their business to challenge government policy. I do not, however, accept the parallel. Notwithstanding the loyalty of a civil servant to the government, his conscience should clearly require him to oppose actions which are either unlawful, unconstitutional, or which involve some great affront to human values. In the last analysis he must be prepared to resign his appointment. But in such circumstances, I believe he should be relieved of his normal obligation to refrain from commenting on policies for which he may have drafted official advice. But all this is to decribe an exceptional situation. What the basic doctrine means, and it is important to understand this, is that the Civil Service cannot be thought of as an in-built safeguard against what some people might call the excesses of a radical or reforming government. The only effective safeguards, if it is safeguards we are seeking, have to be found in the political and judicial processes, or in the force of circumstances themselves – and let me say parenthetically that I have usually found that force of circumstances is the most effective safeguard of the three.

There are however those who doubt whether

officials can be relied on to live up to the code I have described, and who wonder whether a permanent Civil Service is not bound to turn into some sort of priesthood: ignorant of the realities of the wider world, out of touch with the mood of ordinary people and wedded to its own value systems. These critics have suggested that appointments to senior positions in departments should be made of political nominees. An incoming administration would not be saddled with all the officials already in post, but would be able to staff the top jobs with people who had been associated with the new ministers and with the formulation of policy in opposition. In this way, it is argued, departments would be given a strong steer in the direction of the new policy, and this would reduce the danger that officials would successfully obstruct its implementation. There would also be a better chance of maintaining the momentum of the new policy. All too often, it is said, policies lose their impetus as ministers become burdened with the day-to-day business of running their departments, while lukewarm officials see the opportunity to allow 'dangerous' initiatives to die of inanition. If this argument were valid, the introduction of political appointees free from the cares of ministerial office would undoubtedly help to sustain the thrust of policy.

Before I deal with the political case for a development on these lines, let me question whether the appointment of outsiders would lead to a more outward-looking Civil Service. I and my former colleagues have long been exercised that Whitehall should be sensitive to public opinion and aware of the best practices of management outside. I believe that the system we have developed of secondments, of sabbatical absences, of interchange with other employment is beginning to generate a body of officials which is as responsive to outside influences as any in the rest of the world.

However, leaving aside the question whether the Civil Service is as outward-looking as ideally it should be, I have considerable doubt, if the aim is to introduce a greater political element into our Civil Service, whether we would best achieve this by having political appointees as part of the administrative hierarchy (as happens in the American system) or by having them as special advisers working with permanent officials, but not directly responsible for the implementation of policy. The system of special advisers is the one which has been developed in this country, particularly in the past twenty years, and it is now well established. I have no doubt that it is the better course. And I do not say this with the implication that it is the lesser of two evils. I positively believe that politically committed special advisers have a key role in the help a department gives to its minister. They have a very special function in ensuring that the party political dimension of policy-making is fully taken into account at every working level in a department. They can also help the politically neutral officials to appreciate the subtleties and details of party policy to which they may well have contributed when it was worked out in opposition.

By contrast, a system in which political appointees automatically took over the top administrative posts in departments is open to a lot of objections. First, it would severely diminish the appeal of a career in the

Civil Service, to which we surely want to continue to attract some of our brightest young men and women. No-one, I think, is challenging the view that public administration is a vital function in our society and that we need competence at every level. I am convinced that if the opportunities to occupy the highest posts were denied them, the morale of our Civil Service would be impaired, and many who now think in terms of a public service career would turn elsewhere. This would have adverse consequences for the whole administration: its effect would be felt at every level. In the second place, it would lead to the sort of administrative chaos which so often marks a new administration in the United States.

It has been my experience to work with the senior members of several American administrations and I have always been struck by the time it takes them to settle into the unfamiliar environment of Washington and to learn the craft of executive government. This is in no way to criticise them. As businessmen or academics they cannot be expected to know how to run a government department any more than a civil servant can be expected to manage an industrial concern without a lot of training and experience. The mechanics, the procedures and methods of government, the constraints of the administrative process, all these things are new to outsiders; and because they are not familiar with them they make mistakes which experienced hands would not. One of the virtues of the British system is that we change governments smoothly, without the violent dislocation which is a feature of the Washington scene. It is the senior Civil Service's job to make sure that the transition takes place without a hitch, and it is to its credit that the record has been so good.

But there is another reason for hesitating before we politicise our top administrative posts, and it is this. The time-horizon over which policy is formulated would become markedly biased towards the short-term. One of the advantages of a permanent cadre of heads of departments is that their very permanence inclines them to take the long view of the problems they are dealing with. They have to live with the consequences of decisions, often for many years. By contrast a minister's average stay in office is no more than about two years, and the political system under which he operates forces him to seek quick returns on anything he does. I saw many examples of ministerial indifference to reforms where the pay-off would have come only after a lengthy interval. Let me illustrate the point with an example. For many years officials in several departments have been concerned about the inefficiencies and misallocations generated by our system of housing finance, with its restrictions, its subsidies, its tax exemptions and so on. This system was originally justified fifty and more years ago by the considerable social benefits (what economists call 'externalities') which come from good housing, compared with the benefits to be derived from alternative ways of spending money. But as time passed, the trade-off between housing and other objectives of policy has changed, and with it the optimal balance of policy. But it has always been difficult to interest politicians in reform because of the slow rate of social pay-off, compared with the short-term political costs of change.

57

I talked earlier on about the relations between civil servants and their political chiefs and I stressed the importance of trust. But there is one aspect of this relationship which has always worried me: can it become too cosy, too intimate from the point of view of efficiency? And what are the risks if it does?

It is difficult to convey to someone who has not experienced it how close a permanent secretary and a minister can become. A minister's job is a lonely one and his colleagues are not always his close friends and confidants. Indeed they are sometimes rivals, on whom he cannot always rely for disinterested help and advice. By contrast, a senior official has no political ambitions and has a deep personal commitment to the success of his chief. They spend a lot of time together and share intimate thoughts. If the official's judgment is respected he comes to play a bigger part in policy formulation than any of the minister's political colleagues. This can happen even with Prime Ministers, and many of you will remember Lord Feather's description of Lord Armstrong as 'the deputy Prime Minister'. This may have been unfair, but it reflected the important part played by the head of the Civil Service in advising the Prime Minister. In another context, some of the most important economic decisions of the past fifteen years have been taken by the Prime Minister of the day and the Chancellor, supported only by one or two senior officials from the Treasury and the Bank of England. Small wonder that arrangements like these create difficulties for those ministers in the Cabinet who feel they have legitimate claims to be consulted.

But if very close relations between politicians and

civil servants can bring their problems, incompatibility between a permanent secretary and his minister has, in my experience, been more troublesome. This problem can occur when a minister inherits his top adviser from his predecessor. The present conventions make it difficult for a minister to remove his permanent secretary, partly because of the desire of all concerned not to appear to be using appointments for the purpose of patronage, and partly because there is rarely another post to which the permanent secretary can be moved. In spite of these difficulties, I have no doubt that if incompatibility does arise, the minister should be able to remove his permanent secretary.

The relationship, then, between a permanent, politically neutral and meritocratic Civil Service and the small political directorate of ministers which oversees it is crucial both to the successful working of our system of government and to its ability to respond to democratic pressures. Both sides must be sensitive to the dangers and pitfalls to which they are exposed. And above all, the country must be assured that the relationship is a healthy one. I do not really believe that it wants to have Sir Humphrey in the driving seat.

LECTURE 4

Critical Opposition
– Part of the Polity

When Simon de Montfort summoned representatives from the shires and the towns in the year 1265, his aim was to gain the support of the common people in a bid to counter the growing defection of the nobles from his cause. His concern was not to share his power, but to retain and strengthen it. That first parliament is a far cry from the one we know today: a parliament whose prime duty is to curb and control executive power.

But how effective is Parliament today at exercising the functions of supervision and control which the seventeenth-century reformers allotted to it? The model of a supreme assembly, so well described by Bagehot and Mill, does not correspond to the parliaments we have seen for most of the twentieth century. The emergence and strengthening of the party system have given the central government immense authority over the House of Commons. When I joined the Civil Service, I was forcibly struck by the difference between the formal respect I was taught to pay to the parliamentary system and the cavalier way in which Whitehall, for the most part, took the House of Commons for granted.

Fortunately, the last few years have seen something of a parliamentary reaction to the growth of executive power. But party loyalty still acts as a forceful check on parliamentary enthusiasm, and this was strikingly demonstrated earlier this year, when the attempt of a large, all-party group of back-benchers to give Parliament a greater role in the oversight of the nationalised industries collapsed in the teeth of ministerial opposition. The whips of the majority party do not hesitate to suppress, if they can, an incipient back-bench revolt. The prospect of ministerial disapproval, and with it the possible forfeiture of appointment to a government post, act as a powerful sanction on the ordinary MP. Parliament's new desire to oversee the executive can only be welcomed, because the situation that had developed was inimical both to the efficiency of government and to its responsiveness to public opinion, expressed through its representatives. The muting of external criticism and the freedom from the obligation to justify policy *in detail* to some external investigative body, makes for a lack of rigour both in thought and action. It involves a risk that decisions will be taken, which even if they are accepted by Parliament under the threat of party discipline, may not be accepted by the country at large. Above all, it is liable to create a sense of alienation between the government and the governed. So some reversal of the trend of the past century is overdue.

But there is a practical limitation to what the House of Commons can do as a full assembly to scrutinise the executive. A great deal of its time is devoted to three or four main activities: to the examination of bills and subordinate legislation which have simply got to be passed; to the voting of supply; to general debate like foreign affairs and economic policy; and to the discussion of those issues of importance which inevitably arise out of the blue in any session. This is the stuff of the House of Commons as a whole, and it is crucially important to the functioning of a parliamentary democracy. But it involves only general oversight of the executive. Valuable as this is, it is no substitute for the detailed oversight of the sort that keeps a whole administration on its toes. How can Parliament best exercise this detailed oversight? Question Time offers one opportunity to interrogate ministers. But although this serves as a safety valve against arbitrary government, it is not the occasion for the careful explanation and defence of policy or even the justification of individual acts of government. Parts of Question Time have become little more than a parliamentary exercise for the demonstration of ministerial virtuosity and back-bench ingenuity.

It is outside the forum of the whole House that we must seek the opportunities for the development of parliamentary power, and it is here that some of the most important and exciting of recent developments have taken place. I am thinking particularly of the establishment of the Select Committees which now watch over the activities of identified government departments.

The principle of the Select Committee is not a new one, but in the past the number of standing committees has been kept small and they have been confined to such specific issues as parliamentary procedure, the financial estimates, the nationalised industries, and so on. Many of these committees have registered notable achievements in focusing attention on the activities of government and its agencies. The most distinguished has been the Public Accounts Committee, whose function is to call departments to account for their spending. It does this on the basis of reports which are produced by a senior official, the Comptroller and Auditor General, following the presentation each year of the government's accounts. It is a long-established convention that the Committee does not challenge the policies which give rise to the spending. Rather it concentrates on administrative issues, usually specific acts of government: was the expenditure on some item incurred economically and effectively? Did it achieve its particular objective? The principal witnesses are civil servants, usually the permanent head of the department concerned.

The Public Accounts Committee has a formidable reputation in Whitehall, and it commands great respect from civil servants. It is well briefed and fully equipped to examine witnesses. I can assure you that few permanent secretaries who have to go before the Public Accounts Committee will allow themselves any private engagements in the immediate run-up to an appearance. Although the Committee is concerned primarily with economy and effectiveness, its achievements have not been confined to the uncovering of inefficiencies and shortcomings in government administration. One of its great monuments was the pioneering work it did in 1972 on the taxation of the oil companies operating in the North Sea. It was this work which in due course ensured that the nation got its proper share of the benefits from our oil resources.

The success of the Public Accounts Committee lies essentially in its ability to function as a reasonably unified group of parliamentarians, jealous of the role of Parliament as a guardian of the taxpayer and the citizen. They do not behave like a group of politicians driven to fight each other on the basis of party loyalty. This is a most important point, which I will come back to in a moment.

The new departmental Select Committees operate quite differently. Their establishment, in 1979, was the outcome of an explicit decision by the Conservative Party in opposition, which was then confirmed after its success in the General Election of that year. It is true that the idea of departmental committees sprang from the report of the Select Committee on Procedure in 1978, but it would certainly not have been implemented but for the benevolence of the new government. The motive for that benevolence would make an interesting subject for discussion, but it is not one I propose to pursue here.

The committees have differed in their interpretation of how best to carry out their duties, and have adopted a variety of different styles. Many have produced quick, short reports in order to add something to current controversy, or to influence an imminent debate in the whole House. Some committees have felt that their most useful role was to get the facts on the record as quickly as possible, taking evidence on a particular issue from the principals concerned and publishing it without comment. One of the most valuable services which the committees have decided that they can render is to generate a steady flow of factual information to the House, information which would not have been made available by the executive unprompted. The committees claim a number of successes in influencing policy or changing the procedures of the executive. They instance the new Treasury publication, 'The Autumn Statement', a document which gives the House of Commons a financial review at mid-year comparable to what the Chancellor presents at Budget time. They also lay claim to the amendment of the 'Sus' law, and the exposure of the extent of Ministry of Defence disinformation during the Falklands campaign. But the committees believe that their influence is of a more continuing, if perhaps less noticeable kind. As they put it in a combined report issued last year:

> The Civil Service has been widely exposed to parliamentary examination. . . . Equally significant is the deterrent effect on the government of the new arrangements — the knowledge that members are now able, at short notice, to enquire into anything that may arise in the administration of departments.

Well, the committees can perhaps be expected to take a somewhat self-congratulatory view of their activities. But how does Whitehall, from its admittedly partisan standpoint, regard their performance?

Whitehall's instinctive prejudices were evident from the moment that the idea of departmental committees was first put forward in 1978. There was a body of opinion which saw some possible value in the existence of a new platform from which departmental policies could be explained and justified. But many civil servants, including, I regret to say, myself, viewed the development with concern, because we expected the committees to delve into matters which, for apparently good reasons, had been kept confidential, and because too we were apprehensive that officials under public examination would become politically exposed. There is a strong belief in Whitehall that the principle of a politically neutral Civil Service dictates that its members should never be seen in public to be associated with any controversial issue.

In the event, most of these fears have not been realised. The anxiety that civil servants would become identified in public with ministerial policies has been allayed by the committees' separation of policy questions — which they have mostly reserved for ministerial witnesses — from questions of fact and analysis — which have formed the basis for their examination of officials. There have been few breaches of the convention that officials' advice to ministers on policy is privileged and confidential. None of the facts which the committees have elicited from their studies, even including those in the delicate area of defence and foreign policy, has harmed the national interest.

The existence of the committees has, on the other hand, had a number of what I regard as beneficial effects on policy-making. Some of these I had frankly not foreseen.

The first has been the impact on the thinking of ministers and civil servants: the knowledge that your department is going to be examined *in detail* on the background to a policy statement is a great encouragement to be rigorous in formulating your justification for it. And this has indeed happened. If there is evidence or argument which runs counter to a policy decision, departments now have to be prepared to meet that evidence and argument head on, and in public. I have seen the effect of this discipline on the Treasury, as we prepared policy statements like the Budget or, a more precise example, the statement in June last year on the overfunding of public sector debt. One question became commonplace: 'How do we explain this particular awkward fact to the Select Committee?' A further beneficial effect has been to oblige Whitehall to publish more information — information about policy, about expectations and about judgments. Again, to quote from my own experience, the Treasury Select Committee is entitled to credit for drawing from the government estimates of the revenue from North Sea oil tax, forecasts of the likely course of manufacturing output, and a number of important assumptions upon which economic policy is founded. I do not believe there is any valid reason for withholding this sort of information from the public, but I very much doubt if it would have been made available if the Select Committee had not pressed for it.

To take another benefit, I think that whenever ministerial decisions are plainly questionable, their weakness is now more likely to be exposed by the committees than was possible when the debate and questioning were largely confined to the floor of the House. What is more, the very existence of the committees has sharpened the focus for public debate. Their prestige and authority enable them to command contributions on chosen issues, not just from government departments, but from all interested parties, including some from abroad. This has certainly been the case with the Treasury Committee, most notably in its study of monetary policy. Although its report left a great deal to be desired, the background papers which it requested were invaluable to public understanding of this complex issue.

But if these are the beneficial effects, the actual performance of the Select Committees has not to my mind been very impressive. The examination of witnesses has been superficial. The committees have allowed themselves to be sidetracked by evidence which was not relevant to their inquiry. Officials who wanted to stone-wall have rarely had difficulty in doing so and they have been surprised to encounter so little forensic skill. Too often the committees have failed to prepare themselves adequately for the examination, particularly where the subject matter has been general. And as a result, they have wasted valuable opportunities to explore the strengths and weaknesses of a departmental position. On occasion, they seem to have allowed their special advisers to determine the form of the examination, simply reading out prepared questions which they themselves had not understood. Some of their special advisers seem to use the committees as a means to assert a purely personal viewpoint, or to elicit information of value to themselves rather than to the committee. Nor have the committees been greatly interested in issues which have long-term importance. In this respect, their performance is in marked contrast to that of the House of Lords Committees which, while perhaps taking a more leisurely approach, have been willing to delve into unglamorous matters which have important, long-term implications.

How then could matters be improved? One possible way forward would be for the Select Committees to hold more private and informal meetings with official witnesses. At present, the knowledge that every word uttered is on the record and liable to be quoted, acts as a powerful inhibitant on frankness and spontaneity. I myself learned the lesson of caution after a committee appearance at which I was asked without notice to give an estimate of a specific and rather difficult issue. Under strong, and, as I thought, unreasonable pressure, I gave a tentative and necessarily unconsidered view of the matter. That view was subsequently incorporated in the committee's report and came to be quoted by commentators years later as though it had been my considered judgment. Of course, informal proceedings are no substitute for formal sessions, but they would at least offer an opportunity to the committees to understand those aspects and nuances of policy which government witnesses find difficult to express in public and on the record.

I also think that the committees should look closely at their staff support and at the quality of the briefing they receive. They have nothing comparable to the assistance which the Public Accounts Committee has from the Comptroller and Auditor General. I am not advocating large staffs on the model of congressional committees in America. But some strengthening of politically uncommitted advisers would pay handsome dividends. The committees should be wary of advisers with strongly entrenched views.

But there is something more important than the formality of the setting or the strength of their support. The committees need to ask themselves what degree of commitment they are prepared to give to their work. Attendances have sometimes been poor and the mastery of the briefing inadequate. An MP is not always of course a full-time politician, and he has to give a lot of his parliamentary time to his constituents and to any particular issue he may concern himself with. Moreover, he does all this with nothing like the staff support the American congressman has.

Nevertheless, if MPs wish to make a success of the new Select Committee system they will have to see membership as a significant call on their time. Their attitude will be determined by the effect of active committee membership on their political prospects, and on this we have little evidence to date. I confess I think it unlikely that many MPs will see membership, or even the chairmanship of a committee, as a political goal in itself. This factor will inevitably have implications for the way MPs carry out their committee duties.

Any assessment of the potential of the Select Committee system must recognise the limits to what Parliament can achieve in supervising the executive. Much of the intellectual inspiration for the new arrangements came from the other side of the Atlantic, where congressional committees have formidable powers, and play a substantial part in the formulation of government policy. I do not believe that our parliamentary committees can or should aspire to such a position, partly because we do not enjoy the full separation of powers that is a feature of the American constitution, but mainly because of the shadow of the party whip and party discipline

73

which is cast over the British Member of Parliament.

This shadow is a factor which constantly recurs in any examination of Parliament's relationship to the executive. If a Select Committee chooses to study some aspect of public policy upon which the government and the opposition are divided, it is almost inescapable that the members of the majority party will rally to the defence of the government, and the opposition members will unite in condemning it. I have in mind, for example, the occasions when the Treasury Select Committee examines the Budget, for instance, or the role of monetary policy. On both these issues there were, and still are, sharp party differences. The Committee, and especially its chairman, know that a rigorous and unrestrained analysis of the issues would bring out strongly differing views among the members of the Committee, according to their party affiliation. This would lead the Committee in its examination to reveal its internal divisions and to become side-tracked from its principal objective, that of questioning government witnesses. The last thing the members want is a domestic quarrel, with their official witnesses from Whitehall watching like amused bystanders.

The committee system does, of course, impose costs on administration. The committees profess to having concern not to ask for more evidence than is essential. But the time and the effort Whitehall has devoted to servicing committees are substantial. Moreover, these financial costs represent the expenditure of scarce resources, namely the skills and time of busy people, including ministers. But no-one can pretend that these costs are disproportionate to the gains which the committee system has produced and in relation to the costs of the American congressional committees they are infinitesimal.

Now, after this catalogue of advantages and disadvantages, I should make my own view quite clear. The Select Committees have an immensely valuable part to play in getting at the facts and the analysis which underlie policy, and they have the potential to perform well in the reviews of the actions and policies of ministers and departments, provided these are not the subject of acute party controversy. But, for the burning issues of the day, the only effective forum for debate is the House of Commons as a whole, where the principal thrust of criticism and examination must come from the main opposition parties and in particular from their front benches.

In so far as a healthy democracy requires an effective official Opposition its resources should be commensurate with the job it has to do. At present, no provision is made from public funds beyond the ordinary secretarial assistance, to which all MPs are entitled. Financial help comes only from party funds, from interest groups who see in the opposition a champion of their cause, and to a limited extent from charitable foundations. By the standards of the resources available to ministers these are exiguous, and this is reflected in the quality of debate and criticism.

The principal deficiencies of the official opposition are those of staff support, though there are deficiencies of information too. The Select Committees, and the greater flow of information from the executive which now takes place, have gone some way to help, but the Opposition still has precious little back-up for the development of its criticism and questioning. It also lacks the resources to make objective appraisals of the consequences of its own policy alternatives.

The development of these policy alternatives is a vital function for an effective Opposition, for it is only by presenting to the electorate the option of something different from the government's pro-gramme that it can hope to obtain office. But constructive criticism of the government's policies is also an important duty, not least to expose their weaknesses and dangers. In neither respect, looking back over forty years, do I think that our Opposition parties have performed well. They have had little difficulty, perhaps too little difficulty, in formulating their own proposals and policies. But the implica-tions of these policies have usually been ill thought-out. And the Opposition has often formed a new administration before its policies have received the full evaluation which should have preceded the closing of options. But by then the commitments have been made and for the time being, we have been forced to live with the consequences. I believe there is a good case in principle for improving the efficiency of the Opposition by providing it with the staff to do its job effectively.

The solution canvassed in some quarters is that we should establish a Department of the Opposition, staffed with people who would be rather like civil servants: they would be at the service of the front bench and their salaries would be paid from public funds. The size of such a department might be measured in terms of perhaps a few dozen policy advisers plus ancillary staff and the annual cost might be of the order of £1 million — a small sum in relation to the cost of Parliament as a whole. Each shadow minister would have in effect a cabinet of officials. Their business would be to keep a close watch on developments in the area of their chief's portfolio. They would provide advice which enabled him to criticise government policy, and they would put forward constructive alternative proposals. There ought also to be a handful of co-ordinating officials, serving the shadow Cabinet as a whole in much the same way that the Central Review Staff, which I talked about in my second lecture, would serve the real Cabinet.

Well, why do we not have such a department? The answer is that there are both political and administrative objections. The chief political difficulty is common to any suggestion that official funding should be given to a political party as distinct from an official body of Parliament. Our system of government does not formally acknowledge the existence of parties, and barring a salary to the leader of the official Opposition it gives no help or recognition to them. Party political broadcasts are the one exception to this rule: but the way they are allocated usually arouses acute dissatisfaction among the smaller parties. So while the idea of a Department of the Opposition might command political support if we had a permanent two-party system, it is bound to create resentment in a multi-party system. And even if we did have a two-party system, the patronage of official help enjoyed by the Opposition would inhibit the emergence of a new party and so entrench and solidify the status quo.

77

There would also be political anxiety in the minds of some Opposition supporters that an official staff would be likely to capture the minds of their front bench and lead them in the direction of pragmatic, non-ideological solutions. I remember a politician once telling me that one of the advantages of going into opposition was that his party shed its Civil Service advisers and, as he put it, 'was able once again to find its soul'. The fear of some people in politics would be that the Opposition staff and the official Civil Service would be keeping in regular contact, and sharing the same sources of information, with the result that they would tend to come up with similar solutions. The political system would surrender to the middle ground. This is not a view I share, because the role I see for advisers is not to define political objectives, but to appraise policies designed to secure the objectives which the politicians set. What applies to the relationship between ministers and their officials would also apply to shadow ministers and their officials. But a more substantial difficulty lies in the nature of the career which could be provided for the staff of the Opposition. What would happen to them when the Opposition won a parliamentary majority and became the government of the day? I find it hard to imagine that the staff would then serve the new Opposition, however willing and able they might be to do this. The problem of developing a working relationship with their new political chiefs might not itself be insuperable. The real difficulty would lie in the unwillingness of the new government to dispense with its old advisers. Ministers form strong attachments to their personal staffs, and the natural desire of a newly appointed minister, taking office after a period in opposition, would be to retain his old advisers. But to bring them into a department and place them in senior administrative positions would be disruptive in much the same way as the filling of administrative posts by political appointees. Moreover, the new staff would be thought of as political appointees, and if there were a further change of government their position would be insecure. They would be expected to resign with their political chiefs and to serve them again in opposition. In short we would have created a political Civil Service, however politically uncommitted in a party sense that service might be.

These difficulties would remain even if the Department of the Opposition were staffed by ordinary civil servants on secondment — rather as the Cabinet Office is now. Such secondments would have to be for a whole parliament, or at any rate the whole lifetime of an administration, because I cannot see ministers or shadow ministers liking an arrangement under which their advisers could be arbitrarily transferred to their political opponents. I once had quite a problem myself when one of my colleagues resigned from the Civil Service to take a political appointment with the Opposition. The episode created a feeling of distinct and understandable unease on the part of my minister.

In spite of all these difficulties I do believe that the cause of effective government would be greatly served if we could strengthen the support given to the official Opposition. What I would like to see is a limited experiment. We would second a small number of civil servants to the Opposition on the

basis of a fixed period of not more than five years
and on the firm understanding that they would then
be returned to the Civil Service, and given a purely
managerial post away from the political stage.
Provided these safeguards were respected, an
arrangement like this would avoid the dangers of
politicisation that I have described, and would give
the Opposition the sort of professional help it needs.
By treating the idea as experimental, we would bring
to the surface any defects it might contain, and we
would be able to revise it if necessary. I believe our
system of government would survive such an
experiment. It might well indeed acquire new life
from it.

LECTURE 5

Opening up Government

On the 13th of July this year, the House of Commons voted by large majorities not to reintroduce capital punishment. Market research surveys at the time, however, showed that the mass of public opinion was in favour of restoration. The wide gap between the popular preference and the preference of our elected representatives is something which should trouble us all: it is symptomatic of some malfunctioning of the democratic process. It does not seem to me to be satisfactory either to say that the representatives should have deferred to the wishes of those they represent, or to claim that they need take no account of their constituents' views – that their duty, once elected, is simply to obey their own conscience.

We need to ask ourselves why there is such a gap between the public and its representatives on this, as indeed on other issues. The gap must result from the different perceptions each of them has of where the public interest lies. And those perceptions differ, in part at any rate, because of differences in the quality of the debate and differences in the information available. Raising the quality of public debate, and providing the public with the material on which to make an informed judgment on matters of public policy are two major requirements if we are to make the government process operate efficiently and responsively.

I referred a moment ago to the public interest. It is a phrase I rarely use, for it conveys the dubious impression that there is some national interest which transcends the interests of us all as individuals. I do not believe in such a concept, and I speak of the public interest only to denote what our collective will as a society would be if we had access to all the relevant facts and we had a consistent and perceived set of value preferences. If there is a public interest, an informed public is the best judge of where it lies.

It is of course an illusion to suppose that the popular approach to public issues could ever be as informed and sophisticated as that of the responsible expert. But it is surely a counsel of despair to write off public opinion on complex issues. When he declared that 'Public opinion is everything. . . . With it nothing can fail. Without it nothing can succeed,' Abraham Lincoln was indulging in a little high-flown rhetoric. But his sentiments rested on firm ground.

The challenge facing any democratic society, therefore, is to secure a more informed public, not least with the aim of eliminating those unhappy gulfs in choices which occasionally open up between those in government and those they represent. This task falls primarily to our political leaders. It is for them to explain and defend their decisions as they are made and to persuade us of the rightness of those decisions. But there is a need of a more continuing nature – a need for governments on a systematic basis to publish the information they possess which will contribute to public understanding of policy issues. But let me disclaim any expectation that the greater availability of information will of itself transform the situation. The haul is a long one and no contribution can be rejected.

Governments, of course, are not by any means the sole source of information on matters of public interest. Pressure groups, independent research bodies, academic workers, all make it their business to see that we are an informed society. The privileged access to information which is often attributed to government can be much exaggerated. Take the case of economic forecasts, which have been a concern of mine for a long time. Before the government decided to release them, it used to be held that the public were seriously deprived of information which could help them to make a judgment on economic policy. There may have been something in this ten or so years ago. But the demand for publication of official forecasts took little account of the existence of independent, non-official forecasts based on much the same factual and analytical material as was embodied in the Treasury's own work. The reliability of most of these independent forecasts was not noticeably inferior to the Treasury's. It is true that if parts of the Treasury forecast are not published, Parliament and the public do not have access to the same information as the government and may not be able to test the internal consistency of policy. But public understanding of policy issues can often be adequate for the purposes of reaching an informed view, even when the information it is based on is not as complete as the government's.

Another qualification I would make about information is really about privacy: the privacy of government decision-taking. There are many who believe that the public's entitlement to know what is decided on its behalf – an entitlement I do not for a moment challenge – extends to an entitlement to know the content of the detailed discussions through which the executive government reaches its decisions. I cannot accept this. In the process of making up its mind on policy a government will examine several options, together with their supporting arguments. All these options save one it will discard, and in presenting its preferred course it will wish to stress the arguments which support it. Its advocacy of its chosen policy could be materially undermined if it were known to have entertained quite different choices, and to have placed weight on arguments it subsequently wished to play down. The doctrine of collective responsibility would be damaged as differences within the Cabinet were made explicit. What the invasion of government privacy would lead to is the conduct of government business by surreptitious means. Ideas would be exchanged in an unrecordable form. Internal debate would be inhibited. Indeed, recent unauthorised leaks of long-term government thinking in the social field seem to have had the effect of stifling discussion in Whitehall. This must surely be inimical to good government.

We need to accept therefore that the internal deliberations of government, the comment and advice which one part of Whitehall gives to another, should be protected by the ordinary rules of privacy.

The interval which should elapse before historians have full access to public papers is something that can be argued about. The present rule is that government documents are not released for thirty years – this being judged to be the interval which has to elapse to free those who participate in government from the embarrassment of seeing their recent thoughts, differences and doubts exposed to public view, and hence to avoid inhibiting the free and trenchant expression of views in Whitehall without which no government can function effectively. Neither of these considerations, in my view, justifies a period of secrecy as long as thirty years. Except possibly in the area of foreign policy, where our relations with other countries may require a lengthy period of discretion, I would favour a much shorter interval, so as to permit historians to carry out documentary research while they still have the chance to talk to those who made policy.

But to return to the question of what may be currently released. It is, I believe, in the field of factual and analytical material that governments could and should play a more constructive part, for it is here that they possess a wealth of data, much of which is not released to the private citizen or to Parliament.

Government departments commission research, carry out surveys, study what is happening in other countries and generally establish a good and thorough informational base upon which to make policy. They also, of course, have a substantial body of incidental evidence from ongoing administration: evidence like the statistics of social security beneficiaries, the income distribution of the tax-paying public, the accuracy of a weapons system and so on. Most of this information would not be readily available to the public, unless the government supplied it. Much of it is of some public interest and it is difficult to see why in a democracy it should not be published.

The record of British governments in publishing this sort of material is by no means a discreditable one, particularly in recent years. What is more, senior civil servants are now willing to expose themselves to public interviews and these give them opportunities to deploy non-partisan information relevant to policy.

Nevertheless, a suspicion exists that departments do not go out of their way to disclose information – certainly information which sits uneasily with the chosen policy. It is unsatisfactory for Parliament to have to rely on its own alertness and astuteness in eliciting material from the government. This state of affairs has aroused interest in some statutory obligation on the government to publish its privileged information or to provide access to its own records.

So far, all British governments have resisted a Freedom of Information Act. But short of providing a statutory right, governments have developed an informal system which inclines more markedly towards publication. The most significant development was the directive in 1976 which the then head of the Civil Service, Lord Croham, issued to all permanent secretaries. This decreed that the background material relating to policy studies and reports would be published unless ministers explicitly decided it would not. It declared that the aim normally would be to publish as much as possible, and that when policy studies were being undertaken the background material should be written in a form that would permit its publication. It was a significant step forward, and the record of the flow of information which is being released is impressive. It was widely welcomed by the press and by other bodies like Justice, particularly that aspect of the directive which placed in the hands of ministers, and not officials, any decision *not* to publish. But critics have rightly noted that the control of information remains firmly in Whitehall's hands and that there is no provision for checking up on, or auditing the observance of the directive. The citizen has to depend on the unsupervised conscientiousness of officials and ministers. There is some reassurance for us in the quantity of material which is now published compared with what was released only five years ago. But there remains concern that the absence of audit will allow backsliding.

This concern is entirely justified. It is not that I believe that officials have consciously sought to evade the terms of the directive; rather the contrary. They have been pleased to see greater opportunities for the publication of their analytical work, especially when it has been possible to give attribution. But the difficulty of writing a piece of analysis in a form that would permit it to be published has sometimes proved to be serious. Fortunately for good administration, the natural disposition of an official is to write without restraint. But the effect of this frankness has been that a significant number of background papers have been found to contain material which, for one reason or another, has militated against publication.

The reasons for deciding against publication have often been nothing more weighty than political embarrassment. Like, I imagine, many of my former colleagues, I have seen a certain amount of departmental analysis which has not fully supported government policy or government statements about the effects of policy. A quiet decision not to publish has then been the easy way out. One of the safeguards which commentators saw in the 1976 directive — the placing of the responsibility for the decision *not* to publish on ministers — while well-intentioned, has turned out to be based on a fallacy. In my experience ministers are far more apprehensive than their official advisers about the threat to policy that the publication of damaging or unsupportive material can pose. Officials tend to take a more sceptical view about the vulnerability of policy to factual material which is inconsistent with it. And if the material is systematically unsupportive, officials are more likely to wish to see a change of line than their ministerial superiors, who may well have invested a lot of personal political capital in the policy they are pursuing.

But if openness is the aim, are there any limits to the material which, in a democracy, should be more or less automatically released to the public? Clearly in the field of defence and, to a lesser extent, foreign relations, there might have to be some withholding provisions. It would be damaging to national security to give all the performance details of a new weapons system. On the other hand, an informed debate on defence issues can only take place on the basis of such information, and governments ought to strike a reasonable balance between openness and security even here. It is outside the area of national security that I see little cause to be restrictive about publication. It is often argued that the disclosure of some material would be damaging because of its effect on public expectations or on the public acceptance of government policy. Forecasts of unemployment for instance, have been regarded as likely to strengthen opposition to a tough economic programme and to impair its prospects of success. And the same arguments have been used about forecasts of inflation. It was argued in 1976, for instance, that the disclosure of a very high inflation forecast following the fall in the exchange rate that year made the position of trade union leaders difficult in securing their members' acquiescence in the government's pay norm. In another area, the release of key economic information, such as the financial operations of the Bank of England in the foreign exchange market, has been thought to be potentially harmful to those operations, for instance, by revealing market tactics and policy objectives. Having lived with these dilemmas for a very long time, I have become profoundly sceptical about the arguments for secrecy. Step by step over the years we have published more and more material which previous generations of officials had thought to be dangerous. In the event publication has caused very little, if indeed any damage. The onus, I now believe, ought to lie heavily on those who oppose publication to justify their opposition.

Furthermore, I believe it may now be unwise to leave entirely to ministerial discretion decisions about publishing information which would otherwise be available only to government. I hinted a moment ago at the possibility of audit. An alternative approach would be to give the public the right of access to official files, subject to certain limited safeguards.

Let me look at the idea of audit first of all. It is an attractive one, because it would ensure that ministers were not judges in their own cause. Like financial audit, it would provide the public with an independent judgment about the propriety of an executive decision. The procedure would have to be that of audit and not of appeal, because appeal against a ministerial decision is possible only when the decision is known, and a decision not to publish is not usually known. To be effective, an audit would require staff with full access to official files. The auditors would be empowered to make reports to Parliament whenever they encountered a decision not to publish or not to make publicly available factual and analytical material which did not satisfy the criteria for exemption. The staff themselves would not be able to disclose the information, but they would be able to alert Parliament to its suppression and to oblige the minister concerned to defend his decision before the relevant Select Committee, if need be in closed session.

The hope, and indeed the expectation, would be that the existence of audit in the information field, as in the financial field, would ensure that the government rigorously lived up to its stated intentions. The number of occasions where an auditor raised objections could well be small and I suspect that governments would find it a more workable system than they might think.

But keen as I am to see more obligations laid on the government to publish, I have to acknowledge some serious impediments in the way of an external audit system. It would be costly in terms of manpower, even if it operated, like financial audit, on a sample basis. Even more important than this, it might actually become an inhibiting factor in the minds of those who gather factual and analytical material. Departments which feared that some evidence could turn out to be inconsistent with policy might be tempted not to collect it. Ministers might expressly forbid the carrying out of certain research. This may sound fanciful, but I have, I fear, experienced a number of cases, even under the present system, where ministers have been much exercised over research done without their full knowledge, and where the findings have not supported their policy statements. To compound this tendency would be damaging to the convention in Whitehall which happily still permits a large degree of freedom to officials in the assembly of factual material. Then there are the practical difficulties which the auditors would face when they came across material which was partly factual and partly advisory. Nevertheless the idea of an information audit is worth pursuing, and if I am not prepared at present to recommend it wholly without reservation, I do believe it merits serious study.

Our progress towards a more open society now lags behind that of several other mature democracies. They, however, have not chosen the route of audit: instead they have laid a duty on the executive to provide facilities for the citizen to inspect official files. The Scandinavian countries have well-established open systems, the Swedes since the eighteenth century. The United States Congress passed its Freedom of Information Act in 1966. Australia, Canada and New Zealand have all followed the American lead. That so many countries have decided on this course encourages the belief that it is a workable solution. 'Workability' is a test that must be applied to any administrative system, and it is worth looking at how our sister democracies operate their procedures and what their effect has been.

The broad provision of the legislation is to enable the citizen on request to see both the documents generated by a government department and those received by it. Once the citizen has access he is free to publish what he finds. Broad public dissemination therefore tends to take place through the press, rather than by the executive government publishing the material itself. All the schemes enable the executive to protect certain documents, notably those connected with defence, security and international relations, as well as Cabinet papers, working papers and advice from officials. They also allow for the protection of information concerning a citizen's private affairs: tax payments, criminal records and so on. Commercial secrets, too, may be withheld from the public.

These procedures and the exemptions that are permitted, have allayed the anxieties of those who feared the damaging effects of too much exposure. And they seem not to have led to any significant impairment of the efficiency of governments. They have, of course, involved substantial costs to government. The Americans estimated that in the first year of operation, their running costs amounted to $37 million, quite apart from the expenses of litigation and of the time of the officials who have had to carry out the screening of documents.

The critical question has been that of enforcement and review, matters which are crucial to the effectiveness of any scheme. The way countries have tackled this has turned on whether they have a constitution modelled on our own parliamentary democracy, or whether they have a well-developed system of administrative law, as we have not. In the former case, the overriding principle of the account-ability of ministers to Parliament has led to the grievances of the citizen over the withholding of information being argued about and resolved in the political arena. In Scandinavia, by contrast, redress lies by way of appeal to the Ombudsman and finally to an administrative court.

It is perhaps still too early, and in any case presumptuous of an outsider, to assess how far freedom of information by statute has led to any improvement in public enlightenment where it has operated. The changes seem to be small and to fall rather short of what the advocates of more open government would like to see. On the other hand, in the area that I know best, that of economic policy-making, the publication of the minutes of the Federal Reserve Open Market Committee has enabled the whole world to see what criteria determine American interest rates and this know-ledge has had a significant effect on market behav-iour. But the rights created in favour of the citizen have perhaps a deeper significance. What they have done is to go some way to diminish the suspicion, so dangerous to the functioning of democracy, that the executive government is unwilling to be frank and open with the people it represents.

I have spoken so far about the duties of executive government to promote public understanding of policy issues. But there are limits to what government itself can do, since the main channels of public information lie outside the government's hands. I am referring to the press, radio and television. I should be going well beyond the boundaries of these lectures if I were to try to define the responsibilities of the media. Such definition would come more aptly from someone with experience of them. But the frontier between the media and executive government does come within the ambit of my study. The relationship between these institutions is never an easy one, for a free press – if it is to be a bulwark of liberty – must be as vigilant of the government as Parliament itself, and a degree of tension may be inevitable. But in some respects misunderstanding and mistrust between them go further today than is either necessary or desirable.

At present there is an element of abuse of each by the other and a mutual resentment of that abuse. On the side of government, it consists of the manipulation of information. And on the side of the media, it is a degree of unscrupulousness in the publication of official material which has come to them in an unauthorised way.

The manipulation of the media by government chiefly takes the form of the deliberate and covert briefing of selected elements in a way calculated to influence or condition public opinion ahead of some announcement. In its least objectionable form, this briefing may be the provision of privileged information on a non-attributable basis. The effect of such briefing, if it is done skilfully, is to diminish the shock or impact of some disagreeable policy statement. Public opinion is carefully prepared so as to reduce the risk of an immediate adverse 'gut' reaction which might be prejudicial to the policy. No-one can reasonably object to this in principle. The duties of government include the duty of leading public opinion, and the history of democracy is punctuated with instances of great leaders preparing the public for policy changes. But the preparation should, in my view, be an open one, in which ministers freely and explicitly discuss the issues, invite comment and meet criticism. Whatever the ethics of accurate briefing aimed at the conditioning of public opinion, there can be no justification for the use of misleading information. But this is not an unknown phenomenon. If a controversial measure is to be introduced, the hostility of the initial reaction may be tempered by inducing an expectation that something still more unpopular and controversial is in prospect. When reality proves to be milder than expectation, public reaction will be one of relief rather than hostility. When journalists are misled in this way, they become highly suspicious of those who employ the technique. If it were used systematically it would be self-defeating. But occasional, judicious and discreet use can be successful; and it is to be deplored.

I do not wish to imply that the practice is common: I do not believe it is. But the executive government in my view would always be well advised to eschew these practices. I doubt very much if they can be countered by a formal code, to which it would be all too easy to pay token lip service. The remedy lies in the ethos of government. There must be a conscious desire not to be devious, and there can be no better driving force for this desire than the realisation that, in the long run, deviousness breeds distrust, cynicism and eventually contempt.

But if I have been severe in my strictures of certain informal techniques used by government, I am just as critical of the media in respect of some of their practices. I refer to their unhesitating use of official material which comes to them in a blatantly unauthorised way as the result of a leak. I do not propose to go into the moral case for leaks, except to say that in no circumstances could I defend the behaviour of officials who, because they disagree with policy, release information which is calculated to undermine it. Until the rules are changed, the decision to release lies with ministers and ministers alone. But what of the position of the journalist who passively receives unauthorised information? Where does his duty lie? His reply would be: to publish, provided he is satisfied that the material is authentic. Some journalists would perhaps acknowledge a higher duty, if the information were likely to be gravely prejudicial to the national interest in time of war. I remember discussing with a journalist, at the time of the Falklands conflict, what his reaction would be if he obtained simultaneously a copy of our order of battle and a copy of the government's negotiating brief for the annual farm price review in Brussels. He said he would suppress the former and publish the latter.

I wonder whether he should have been so clear-cut

in his views. In both cases publication would have been damaging to the public interest even as I have defined it, and if journalists are prepared to admit to the existence of the public interest in one instance I do not see how they can so easily dismiss it in another.

The leak is a blatant breach of the rules under which we play the game of government. What I have said in this lecture puts me firmly on the side of those who would like to see more openness. But the proper route to openness is by changing the rules, not by breaking them. A journalist who connives at their breach is contributing to the undermining of confidence in government no less than the perpetrator of the leak himself. To this the journalist will reply that the pressures of competition oblige him to use a 'story', however he gets it. If he does not, a competitor will and his own publication will lose circulation. He will no doubt add that the present system does not easily distinguish authorised briefings from unauthorised leaks. And finally he will argue that he is not a party to the rules whose observance I wish to see respected. The rules of disclosure are rules devised by politicians for their own use. If a journalist is to be asked to obey rules he should have a voice in their definition.

These arguments are cogent, but they do not dispose of the issue. Just as governments would gain from the abandonment of devious practices against the media, so I believe that the media should ask themselves whether they really promote democracy and enlightenment when they seek exposure at all costs. As with government, any change in practice would have to be a matter of internal self-discipline backed up, perhaps, by the authority of the Press Council. No externally imposed code could work; and to attempt one would be a grave interference with the liberty of the press.

The problems, then, of creating an informed and enlightened public are not easy to resolve. All good democrats can assert their belief in the direction in which we should be travelling. But on this journey, as on so many others where government is concerned, there are few easy short cuts. More important, in my view, than any institutional changes is the need for a commitment on the part of all who work in the field of government positively to want an informed public. If this is lacking, little in the way of machinery will help.

LECTURE 6

Participation –
The Sole Bond

When Aristotle stated that man is by nature a political animal, he was not only seeking to distinguish humanity from the lower animals: he was asserting the importance of the state – or, as we might say, government – in the human condition. And when in Book 3 of *The Politics* he examines what elements go to determine the nature of being a citizen, he explicitly identifies 'participation in giving judgement'. This concept of participation in government is one which ran through a great deal of Athenian political thought and action. The Greek city state, the *polis*, was small enough to permit all free men to share in the taking of political decisions, and it was an important duty laid upon the citizen to accept the responsibility that this entailed. Representative government, as we know it today, would have been a peculiar, indeed a questionable idea. Of course offices of state existed in Athens and their holders had a measure of delegated discretion, but they were often filled by lot and were in any case subject to a degree of popular oversight in their daily actions which governments today would find hard to stomach.

The size alone of the modern state rules out the

Athenian model as one we should try to copy, even if we wanted to. Debate can only be organised in an assembly of a few hundred people and decisions must be entrusted to an even smaller number. And a good thing too, say some. Government, they argue, is a complex and subtle process, which can be understood and operated only by a small elite; the bulk of the citizens in any society are too pre-occupied with their daily problems to want to engage in regular political debate and decision-taking, except perhaps at the local level; why force them to consider affairs of state? Better by far allow them to elect representatives to do their political thinking for them.

This is not a foolish idea, and it has forceful apologists. They hold that government by a small number of people, answerable periodically for their performance when they seek reelection, is more likely to be efficient and wise than government which is perpetually subject to mass popular pressures. Public opinion, they tell us, can never be well-informed or enlightened. It is readily swayed by demagogues and can too easily be led to demand action which is inimical to its own long-term interests. By contrast, the accountable representative has both the time and the inclination to follow and participate in the debate and come to wise and informed conclusions. Despotism is avoided by the obligation laid on him to account periodically for his stewardship, and by the freedom of others to compete for his office.

As a model for democracy I find this seriously deficient. The participation in government it offers to the mass of the populace is minimal. The choice

104

of representative is no substitute for the choice of policy. Conceded such a limited role in determining public issues, ordinary people — as we have seen — have taken the course of bypassing representative government. They have associated themselves with people of similar interests into trade unions, pressure groups and lobbies. They have sought to influence government decisions not primarily by the process of influencing their representatives, but by applying pressure at the very point where policy is made, in executive government. The evolution of pluralist organisations has had its counterpart in the machinery of central government. Departments 'mark' pressure groups and special interests. Even Parliament has now organised itself through its Select Committees in this way. As a result, political decisions at every level of government are reached with a view, in part at least, to satisfying these pressure groups and interests. Whether they satisfy the requirements and aspirations of the rest of us is a question all too rarely asked. The pressure group in fact is often quite unrepresentative of the people as a whole. The costs of deferring to it are rarely evaluated in terms of the impact on the entire community. It is much easier politically for governments to come to terms with some special interest than to oppose it. Those who suffer from the compact are often unorganised, and their protests — if they are ever articulated — go unheard.

I do not want to deny all value to pressure groups. In a pluralist society they provide likeminded people in association with a means of bringing more influence to bear on political decisions than they otherwise could. They constitute an additional route through which executive government can be brought to account for and be made to defend its policies. In that sense they may be conducive to more open government, to the development of more public debate and to the promotion of public awareness of live political issues. Whatever one thinks of the methods and objectives of the Campaign for Nuclear Disarmament, no one can deny that it has performed a public service in focusing opinion on one of the most crucial political issues of the twentieth century.

But if the political influence of pressure groups is to be kept in check, it can only be done by more, not less, popular involvement in decision-taking. There is ample evidence that the public want this. The Kilbrandon Commission on the Constitution found widespread evidence of dissatisfaction with the accessibility of the political system and of a desire for more responsiveness from it. Nor is this a new thought. John Stuart Mill put the point precisely when he argued that the best kind of responsible government is one

> in which public participation is as great as the general degree of improvement of the community will allow. . . . Nothing less can be ultimately desirable than the admission of all to a share in the sovereign power of the state.

The challenge today is to make the representative political process more publicly acceptable. And the key lies in seeking to reestablish the Greek ideal in concept if not in precise form.

It has been one of my central concerns in these lectures to address myself to the task of making government decision-taking efficient. Efficiency is

106

certainly one important criterion for securing public approval of government. But efficiency is not of itself — even if widely interpreted — the only criterion for popular support. A general feeling that government is sensitive and indeed responsive to the public's hopes and desires is an even more critical element in any democracy.

It is partly in recognition of this that governments have done so much in recent years to promote a dialogue between the government and the governed. They consult much more widely than they used to before taking firm decisions on policy. The open consultative document upon which public comment is sought and which forms the basis of a parliamentary Select Committee investigation has become a common feature of the political scenery. Governments get a useful indication of popular feeling, too, from market research surveys of public opinion. These are healthy developments and I am sure they will be taken further. But they have their limitations and they do not bring us much nearer to a participatory democracy. The extent to which governments consult public opinion or seek public comment is still determined by the government itself. And the value of one-off public opinion surveys — based as they have to be on simple and sometimes slanted questionnaires — is not always clear.

The difficulties of determining the popular will apply also to the holding of referenda on issues of public interest, one of the techniques considered from time to time as a means of popular participation, but applied nationwide in this country only once — on the issues of our continued membership of the European Community. The advocates of referenda view them either as a means of checking or promoting constitutional change or of establishing public support for a policy which may be opposed by sectional and influential interests. Although they are widely used in the United States, where at the local and state level the electorate is frequently invited to decide some public issue, and in a more limited way in Europe too, they have not found favour here. The Burkean doctrine of the right of the elected representative to decide issues on behalf of his constituency is deeply entrenched. And our politicians are reluctant to surrender this right. In any case, it is a rare political issue that can be presented to a mass audience in a simple 'either/or' form. Some questions, like the one in 1975 on our continued membership of the European Community, may lend themselves to such treatment. But others, like the issue of capital punishment, do not. To establish a clear view from the electorate of its position on this matter, it would be necessary to define with some care the crimes for whch capital punishment was being considered, what — if any — degree of judicial discretion would be allowed, and so on.

In a parliamentary debate, all these aspects can be deployed at length and Parliament can then reach a precise decision which can be turned into law. A public debate lacks this precision and a public decision can at best be only a general one. Nor can there be much confidence, as things stand, in the public's decision being an informed one. If it is to reach an enlightened view for or against capital punishment, the public should have available a great deal of factual and analytical material. They should, for instance, have statistics of the incidence of the crime, evidence about those who commit it, facts about recidivism, evidence about deterrence, facts too about the circumstances in which capital punishment is administered. But if capital punishment is a difficult issue on which to poll public opinion, how much more complex is a matter like, for instance, the level of National Insurance Benefits. The question 'Do you think that the retirement pension for a married couple should be set at £55 or £60, or £70 a week?' would produce one set of answers. But if the question also spelt out the consequences of each level of benefit – if we were told, for instance, what the insurance contributions for people in work would have to be in each case – the answer would almost certainly be different. Without a good deal of education and enlightenment public opinion, polled in this way, could well be a poor guide to policy – poor not in the sense that it would not correspond to elite opinion, but poor in that it would be ill-informed and in the long run unacceptable, even to those expressing it. The perverse way in which voting takes place on the various fiscal propositions put to the electorate by the State of California is a sufficient illustration of this point. The binding referendum therefore cannot take the place of a parliamentary decision on complicated public issues.

And this brings me to one of the most important aspects of our parliamentary system: the contact between the sitting Member of Parliament and his constituents. How good are our representatives at keeping their finger on the public pulse and could they do more? Most of our members have a good record on this, though the nature of the system of consultation may give them a biased view. The extended length of our parliamentary sessions compared with those of continental assemblies and of the United States Congress limits the time a member can spend face-to-face with his constituents. His weekends are taken up either with surgeries — that is to say sessions at which he hears their grievances, usually of a rather personal kind — or at meetings with his party supporters. Both of these groups, the aggrieved and the partisan, are unrepresentative of the constituency as a whole, and their voices may give a distorted impression of what public opinion in the round really wants.

I used for a while to have meetings with one minister I worked for each Monday morning. He would come back from his constituency with the views and opinions he had picked up there over the weekend. They nearly always consisted of approval of what the government was doing. Yet I knew from national opinion surveys that the government was not enjoying support for the particular action we were taking. The minister was simply being told what it was supposed he wanted to hear. I see no easy solution to this problem. Each MP must, I think, take whatever steps he sees open to him to determine the preferences of his constituents as a whole.

The media, of course, have a major part to play in giving voice to public opinion, but their function is more that of opinion-former than opinion-seeker. They offer a platform to advocates and opponents of particular policies and they provide the route through which the public acquire the information they need to reach a conclusion. But what that conclusion is too often remains obscure. Public opinion will perhaps always be amorphous and indeterminate, except on the greatest and simplest issues of policy. To attempt to systematise a definition and a crystallisation of public opinion may be doomed to failure because of the sheer size of the public and the complexity of most issues.

But if we cannot hope to get more definition and more decision from the public, should we be complacent about the level of public debate and the quality of information to which the public have access? After all, the fact that public opinion may be difficult to measure and assess does not mean that it is unimportant. And if public opinion is important, it is surely important that it is enlightened.

In last week's lecture I talked about the duty of government to make available to the public the factual and analytical material it assembles in the course of formulating policy. This is an important element of public education. But the government is not the sole, or even the primary source of much information and analysis. It would be a sorry thing for democracy if it ever came to depend exclusively on government for information. Fortunately there is little danger of this happening here. Our press and other media have a high standard of professional reporting. We are also endowed as a country, though less so than the United States, with a number of bodies which seek to promote public under-standing of policy issues. These bodies, largely financed from private funds, carry out extensive research into economic, sociological and strategic matters — research which is renowned for its rigour,

111

independence and impartiality. And the contribution they make to the democratic process — and for that matter to the policy-making process — is considerable. But their findings and the conclusions of the discussion they promote do not always percolate to the public at large; nor do they always make the impact that they should when they reach the policy-makers' desks. The present generation of civil servants, if not their predecessors, is aware of the value of empirical research and evidence as a basis for policy-making, and it makes regular use of the research institutes. But there are some politicians of a more ideological cast of mind who are unenthusiastic. Facts can be uncomfortable bedfellows alongside dogmatic conviction.

If there is one medium outside government which has, in the course of our history, succeeded in making an impact on both public opinion and on policy-makers it is the Royal Commission. Other countries have, of course, their own investigating mechanisms, but the Royal Commission here and elsewhere in the Commonwealth is almost unique. It combines authority and prestige with thoroughness of approach: the authority comes from the high status of its members, the thoroughness from its command of resources and the co-operation it receives from the public. Royal Commissions have played a substantial part in shaping our history for nearly a thousand years. They have contributed greatly to the enrichment of public understanding of political issues, particularly when the public conscience was exercised. The spread of issues which Royal Commissions have studied extends from the maintenance of lighthouses to the reform of criminal procedure, from the secondary school system to the slaughtering of horses. Though they usually have power to make recommendations, these are not binding on the government of the day. But a decision to set aside a Royal Commission recommendation is politically awkward, not just because it is embarrassing to reject the considered advice of a prestigious body (and one that the government itself may have appointed) but because the interests which support the Commission's conclusions can be relied on to make maximum political capital out of a rejection. And even in cases where governments have not accepted Royal Commission recommendations, the expository work which the Commissions carry out and publish performs a valuable role in educating opinion. Above all, the work of Royal Commissions gets noticed by the press and by the public generally. The same work carried out unofficially or informally does not attract comparable attention. Even minority reports — as Mr Selwyn Lloyd found on the Beveridge Committee on Broadcasting, when he alone came out in favour of commercial television — can have powerful effects on the development of opinion.

Not everyone in the past has shared my admiration for Royal Commissions. The eighteenth-century jurist, Blackstone, was very critical of their use, and A.P. Herbert, in a typically amusing satire, argued that the appointment of a Royal Commission was evidence of a failure to govern. But perhaps he only meant that the government was sharing power? Royal Commissions, and even their less prestigious cousins, the Departmental Committees, are used fairly sparingly by governments — on average, one

113

Commission and about twenty Committees a year. The motives for setting one up are often confused. The subject matter may be complex and controversial, like industrial relations; it may be new, like cable television; it may be a subject which calls for a good deal of fact-finding; or it may be one where the government feels reluctant to make a move without securing a measure of independent support. Sometimes, alas, the Royal Commission is a device for putting a difficult subject on the back burner. Establishing one, therefore, is a fairly haphazard and arbitrary matter. It would be difficult to detect any system or coherence in the pattern of their appointment.

An important feature of the Royal Commission is that its creation lies in the hands of the government and no-one else. The members, too, are selected by the government. The terms of reference are written by the government. Whitehall invariably spends a good deal of effort defining the remit of an external body, to make quite sure it will not trespass on territory which it does not want explored.

If we ask ourselves why the government should control the establishment, composition and remit of Commissions, the only valid answer is that, as things stand, there is no-one else, except possibly Parliament, to do it. And even if Parliament were the authority for recommending Royal Commissions, the government — through the control it exercises over the House of Commons — would still be in the driving seat. In any case the House of Commons shows a much greater disposition to carry out investigations itself through the Select Committee machinery rather than appoint non-parliamentarians to do the same job. So if the system is to continue in its present form it is probably only the government who can decide.

But leaving to the government decisions to establish Commissions and to determine what they should investigate has many drawbacks and deprives the public debate of much potential material. I can think of many subjects which would merit dispassionate and authoritative investigation, free from party and sectional prejudice. The political supervision of the police, the relevance of our social security system to the problems of poverty and incentive, the financing of higher education — all these come to mind as possibilities. Many of them, of course, are under review by the Select Committees. But as I have already argued in these lectures, the Select Committee, by virtue of its partisan composition and its concern with the short term, does not function at all like a Royal Commission. And even the most enthusiastic upholder of parliamentary sovereignty would find it hard to class a Select Committee report with that of a Royal Commission.

Is there, then, an alternative which would cut the link between the Royal Commission and the government and create exciting new opportunities for independent and statesmanlike investigation of issues of public importance? I believe there is. Instead of the individual *ad hoc* Royal Commission appointed to do a specific job, there would be a single, large, permanent Royal Commission from which panels would be drawn to carry out specific studies. It would be the Commission itself, not the government, which decided what issues to investi-

115

gate, what terms of reference to give its panels and who should sit on them. Though the panels would normally be drawn from the Commission itself, suitable non-members could be co-opted for individual studies. But decisions on co-option would be for the Commission alone. Membership of the Commission would be for a fixed period and would follow appointment by the Crown on the advice of the Prime Minister. The Prime Minister would be expected to give advice not in a partisan or government-biased way. He should be guided by a spectrum of interests and he would be morally bound to take due account in his recommendation to the Crown of nominations made by certain non-government bodies. If, as I would argue, the size of the Commission were thought of in terms of a couple of hundred or so persons, its composition could take in the professions, commerce, industry and banking, education, social work, and so on. It would not be difficult to agree on the range of activities and experience from which appointments would be made, though I would hope that the selection of people would be adventurous and not always 'safe'.

Membership would carry with it an obligation, when requested, to serve on a particular panel and to give the sort of commitment which membership of a Royal Commission always entails. The Commission would have to elect an executive board with a chairman to arrange and conduct its business. All these appointments would be in the hands of the Commission itself and not of the government. The Commission would, of course, need a staff which would have to be both sizeable and competent. They could be career civil servants on secondment, but if this were thought to be creating an undesirable link between the government and the Commission, it might be possible to think of a core of staff that belonged to the Commission alone. The Commission would, within reason, largely determine its own budget, though it would be subject to public audit like all public bodies.

From the description and specification I have given, you can see that in many ways we already have such a body to hand in the shape of the House of Lords. The present second chamber, however, would be unsuitable — not just because of the hereditary principle, but more importantly because membership is for life, and as a result the average age is high. It would be an important feature of the scheme I am proposing that membership of the Commission would not be permanent and that it should embrace relatively young people as well as those with mature experience.

A body like this might be thought to be in competition with the parliamentary Select Committees, but I think in fact it would be complementary to them. The Select Committees have shown themselves to be preoccupied with shorter-term issues and with the preparation of reports for parliamentary debate. These functions would continue and they would not be in conflict with those of the new Commission. Where interests did overlap, I can see no reason why Select Committees should not have a dialogue with the appropriate panel of the Commission.

The concept of a standing, that is, a permanent Royal Commission is not a new one: what is new about this suggestion is the limitlessness of the remit I want to give it. 'Limitlessness' is perhaps a frightening concept. Would the Commission, for instance, be able to look at the constitution itself? How comfortable would we all be if it were to choose to examine such sensitive issues as the disestablishment of the Church of England or proportional representation or perhaps the jury system? I think we would have to accept the risk of such studies, and I for one would be glad to do so. I would expect limitlessness to be tempered by the good sense and statesmanlike qualities of the Commission's members. I would not want them to be too cautious, but I would expect them to be sensible. At the end of the day the safeguard would lie in their having no executive powers. The Commission's role would be strictly analytical and advisory. It would still be for Parliament and the government to decide what to do.

But, having made this suggestion, let no-one suppose I am naive enough to believe that a standing Royal Commission, with wide powers of examination, would transform our system of government. It would at best be one step further along the road to a more open, participatory democracy. Years of experience have taught me to value the small steps along the right road above the great leap forward in the dark. In his essay 'On Compromise', written just over a century ago, John Morley described the wise innovator as the man who had learned how to seize the chance of a small improvement while working incessantly in the direction of greater ones.

It is this thought which, more than any other, has informed my approach to the subject of these lectures. Looking back on nearly forty years' experience of government, I am struck not by its deficiencies, which I have perhaps dwelt on over the past six weeks, but by its strengths. I am struck too by the adaptability it has shown to changing circumstances, always preserving what was best, but being ready to discard what had become obsolete and irrelevant. This evolutionary quality of our system of government reflects our pragmatic and cautious approach as a nation to change and reform. It is an approach I instinctively warm to. But caution and conservatism have their dangers. They can breed complacency and suspicion of change, characteristics on which the worm in the apple of any society feeds voraciously.

The yardsticks I have applied in gauging the need for change have been efficiency and responsiveness: efficiency because of the incessant need for any institution to achieve its objectives at lowest cost to those who have to bear it, and responsiveness because the test of government in any democracy is ultimately its acceptability to those it governs. If responsiveness has gradually gained the upper hand as my talks have unfolded, it is because I have found it the more elusive of the two ideals, and the more difficult to realise. But it is also today the more pressing. As a people we are now better informed, more politically conscious and less willing to accept external authority than has ever been the case throughout our history. Our leaders must recognise these developments and see them not as something to be resisted and opposed, but as a challenge which, by being met, can give new life to our democracy.

This is my answer to those who see in some of my

ideas costly and cumbrous machinery which will slow down and impede the despatch of business and weaken the effectiveness of government. When the authors of the American constitution prescribed their elaborate system of checks and balances, they knew that they were putting obstacles in the way of swift decisions and decisive action. But their instincts were right and two hundred years of history have proved this. The reflections which these lectures have prompted have led me to conclude that we too need our checks and balances, and if the ones I have suggested prove to be inoperable, one day we shall have to devise others. Above all, we must keep alive the sense of a need for change. As Woodrow Wilson said, 'Democracy is like a living thing, always a-making.' We owe it to posterity never to allow the 'a-making' to seize up.